I0162233

The Brothers by James Shirley

A COMEDIE. As it was Acted at the private House in Black Fryers.

James Shirley was born in London in September 1596.

His education was through a collection of England's finest establishments: Merchant Taylors' School, London, St John's College, Oxford, and St Catharine's College, Cambridge, where he took his B.A. degree in approximately 1618.

He first published in 1618, a poem entitled Echo, or the Unfortunate Lovers.

As with many artists of this period full details of his life and career are not recorded. Sources say that after graduating he became "a minister of God's word in or near St Albans." A conversion to the Catholic faith enabled him to become master of St Albans School from 1623–25.

He wrote his first play, Love Tricks, or the School of Complement, which was licensed on February 10th, 1625. From the given date it would seem he wrote this whilst at St Albans but, after its production, he moved to London and to live in Gray's Inn.

For the next two decades, he would write prolifically and with great quality, across a spectrum of thirty plays; through tragedies and comedies to tragicomedies as well as several books of poetry. Unfortunately, his talents were left to wither when Parliament passed the Puritan edict in 1642, forbidding all stage plays and closing the theatres.

Most of his early plays were performed by Queen Henrietta's Men, the acting company for which Shirley was engaged as house dramatist.

Shirley's sympathies lay with the King in battles with Parliament and he received marks of special favor from the Queen.

He made a bitter attack on William Prynne, who had attacked the stage in Histriomastix, and, when in 1634 a special masque was presented at Whitehall by the gentlemen of the Inns of Court as a practical reply to Prynne, Shirley wrote the text—The Triumph of Peace.

Shirley spent the years 1636 to 1640 in Ireland, under the patronage of the Earl of Kildare. Several of his plays were produced by his friend John Ogilby in Dublin in the first ever constructed Irish theatre; The Werburgh Street Theatre. During his years in Dublin he wrote The Doubtful Heir, The Royal Master, The Constant Maid, and St. Patrick for Ireland.

In his absence from London, Queen Henrietta's Men sold off a dozen of his plays to the stationers, who naturally, enough published them. When Shirley returned to London in 1640, he finished with the Queen Henrietta's company and his final plays in London were acted by the King's Men.

On the outbreak of the English Civil War Shirley served with the Earl of Newcastle. However when the King's fortunes began to decline he returned to London. There his friend Thomas Stanley gave him help and thereafter Shirley supported himself in the main by teaching and publishing some educational works under the Commonwealth. In addition to these he published during the period of dramatic eclipse four small volumes of poems and plays, in 1646, 1653, 1655, and 1659.

It is said that he was "a drudge" for John Ogilby in his translations of Homer's Iliad and the Odyssey, and survived into the reign of Charles II, but, though some of his comedies were revived, his days as a playwright were over.

His death, at age seventy, along with that of his wife, in 1666, is described as one of fright and exposure due to the Great Fire of London which had raged through parts of London from September 2nd to the 5th.

He was buried at St Giles in the Fields, in London, on October 29th, 1666.

Index of Contents

To His Truly Noble Friend Thomas Stanley Esq

SIR,

The Memory and Contemplation of good Offices received, which, by their own nature, and impulsion, have inclined other men to bee active in their returnes, have not wrought me into so much boldness; For when I considered my obligation to your favors I was still deterred by their greatness and number; For in my poverty I had thoughts not without Ambition to reach them with some merit, but when I was studying to proportion my gratitude, I fell much lower than when I was the object of your mercy. The way to releeve my self, is no more to look at what you have confer'd, but on the bestower, for I have now learn'd to separate you from your benefits, and to convey my self into your pardon, by the exercise of your Charity. Thus in place of cancelling my former debts, I put your vertue to a new disbursment: Witness this Composition, which after its birth, had in my thoughts a dedication to your name, although it but now took the boldness to wear it in the forehead both as an Ornament and preserver. You were pleas'd to grace it with your fair opinion, when it was represented, and though it appear not in that naturall Dress of the Scene, nor so powerfull, as when it had the soul of action, yet your smile upon it now will give it second animation; by which I shall derive after so long a silence, a Confirmation of my happiness, in being still received

Sir
Your most humble Servant
JAMES SHIRLEY.

DRAMATIS PERSONAE
Don Carlos.
Luys, his Son.
Don Ramires.
Fernando   } Sons to Don Ramires.
Francisco   }
Don Pedro, a Nobleman.
Alberto, a Gentleman, lover of Jacinta.
Theodoro, brother to Don Carlos.
Jacinta daughter to Don Carlos.
Alsimira, a Noble Widow.
Felisarda, Theodoro's Daughter
Physicians.
Notarie.
Confessor.
Servants.

SCENE

Madrid.

THE PROLOGUE

Troth Gentlemen, I know not what to say
Now I am here, but you shall have a play;
I hope there are none met but freinds if you
Be pleas'd to hear me first, I'le tell you true,
I doe not like the Prologue, 'tis not smart,
Not aery, then the play is not worth a—
What witty Prologues have we heard? how keen
Upon the tyme, how tickling o'the spleen?
But that wits gone, and wee in these sad dayes
In corse dull fleam, must preface to our playes,
I'le shew you what our Author meant should be
His Prologue,—Gentlemen, he shall pardon me
I dare not speak a line, not that you need
To fear a satire in't, or wit in deed.
He would have you believe no language good,
And artfull, but what's clearly understood,
And then he robs you of much mirth, that lyes
I'th' wonder, why you laugh at Comedies.
He saies the tymes are dangerous, who knowes
What treason may be wrapt in giant prose,
Or swelling verse, at least to sense? nay then
Have at you Mr. Poet, Gentlemen,
Though he pretend fair, I dissemble not,
'are all betray'd here to a Spanish plot
But doe not you seem fearfull; as you were
Shooting the bridge, let no man shift, or stir,
I'le fetch you of, and two houres hence you may
(If not before) laugh at the plot, and play.

THE BROTHERS

ACT I

SCENE I

A Room in Don Carlos's House.

Enter **FRANCISCO, JACINTA, FELISARDA**.

FRANCISCO
I Take my leave Jacinta, and cannot wish you
More happiness than you possess.

JACINTA
You must

Dissemble, or it is within your wishes
To make you self, Francisco, mine, which would be
A fair addition to me, in my faith
Of that most noble love you have profess'd.

FRANCISCO
When you but dare to own me, I am past
The fear of any destiny that can

[Enter **DON CARLOS** and a **SERVANT**

Divide us—but your Father. Your own virtue
Be still you guard. I do not like this watch
Upon our meeting, pretty Felisarda.

[Exit

DON CARLOS
Tel Signior Francisco I would speak with him.

[Exit **SERVANT**.

I do not like his frequent visites: though
His birth and generous parts deserve to march
With men of honorable name, I am
Without ambition to sacrifise
My daughter to his pension for life.

[Enter **FRANCISCO**.

FRANCISCO
Your pleasure sir?

DON CARLOS
Hath hitherto Francisco
Been to affect you in the list of those
I held my freinds.

FRANCISCO
I hope no forfeit made
By me, hath lost that good opinion
You plac'd upon me.

DON CARLOS
I cannot tell
How you may be transported with desires
Above my thoughts t' allow, I would not have
My silence, and the free access y' have had

To my house, (which still is open to wise guests,)
Betray me, or my Daughter to the mirth
And talk of men i'th' Plassa, My estate
Doth walk upon sound Feet, and though I make
No exception to your blood, or person, sir,
The portion I have fixt upon Jacinta,
Beside the wealth her liberall Aunt bequeath'd her,
Is more than your thin Younger brother's fortune
Should lay a siege, or hope to. I am plain.

FRANCISCO
And something passionate (if I understand you)
Without a cause. I am a gentleman,
With as much sense of honor, as the proudest
Don that doth ride on's foot cloth, and can drop
Gold to the numerous minutes of his age
And let me not be lost for want of that,
Deserves not to be nam'd to fill the ballance
Against true honour—let me tell you sir,
Virtue and blood are weigh'd against themselves,
You cannot know the price of these, when either
Scale is not poiz'd with things of the same nature.

DON CARLOS
Y'are very right, and therefore I do weigh
My Daughters wealth against your fortunes sir,
I take it they are things in the same specie,
And find it easy to distinguish, yours
Can hold small competition, and by
A consequence that Fathers use t' inferre,
As little hope to equall in affections.
Sir I must tell you I esteem Jacinta
Fit every way to meet your Elder Brother,
Whose Birth will interest him so much in that
Full fortune which your Father now is Lord of,
Your expectations may prompt you look
Without much curiositie for a Bride,

FRANCISCO
I shall believe thy soul is made of Atomes,
That placeth so much happiness in Dust.
[aside]
Sir, I can quit your Jealousie, my thoughts
Levell beneath your Daughter, and shall be
Happie if you consent I may devote
My applications to Felisarda, your Neece.

DON CARLOS

Is it my Neece? I ask your pardon.
Nay then be welcome, and t'encourage you,
Although her Father a poor Gentleman
My brother, by the malice of the sea
And winds, have lost what might have rank'd him even
With some that ride upon their reverend mules,
I'll find a portion for her, if you strike
Affectionate heartes, and joy to call you Nephew.
Pray be not angry, that I take a care
To place my own, where I may see it answerd
With State, as well as Family.

FRANCISCO
You shew
A provident Father. I shall not then
B' indanger'd to your scruple, if I address
My services to her, whose humble fortune,
In the relation to your blood, and nobleness,
Is wealth enough to me?

DON CARLOS
I wish it prosper.

FRANCISCO
You have much honor'd me.

[Exit.

DON CARLOS
That scruple's vanish'd.
These are considerings, with which Parents must
Timely prevent the folly, and the fall
Of Children, apt to lose themselves in shadowes
And gaudy apparitions.

[Enter **SERVANT**.

SERVANT
Your Son
Is come from Salamanca Sir.

DON CARLOS
I hope
Philosophy hath by this time tam'd his wildness,
I have been careful not to feed his riots.
He's welcome; my next study is to choose
A wife for him,

SERVANT
With him a Gentleman.
That seems of noble quality.

[Enter **LUYS** and **ALBERTO**.

LUYS
Your blessing,
Next which 'twil be a happiness, if you
Embrace this noble Gentleman Don, Alberto,
To whose affection I have been engag'd.

ALBERTO
Our studies grew together, and our loves.

DON CARLOS
You do an honour to us.

LUYS
If he thrive
Upon his fair intents sir to my Sister,
Whose character he ha's took delight to hear
From me sometimes, it will enlarge our honor.

DON CARLOS
He has improved in language—his estate?

LUYS
Six thousand ducats sir per Annum clear
In his possession, beside
The legacie of a Granam when she dyes
That ha's outliv'd six cats within their family.

DON CARLOS
This tastes again of the old humor, hee's
Not setled yet.

LUYS
Your pardon sir, I cannot
With any patience think of an old woman,
They are agues to my nature, she that lives
To three score is a witch, and fit for fuel
By the Civil law. I hope my mother's well.
Sir I beseech you, be not you mistaken,
I am not what I was, I'm strangely alter'd
From the wild garbe, and can discourse most gravely
Of any thing but old and toothless women.
Do not you think it fit, she should be burn'd sir,

That lives within an Hospital till the roof
Consume to dust, and no more left for covering
Than is kept up in one continued Cobweb,
Through which the birds may see her when she creeps
Under a spiders canopie; what think you?
Speak your own conscience.

DON CARLOS
A young wife will cure
This angry heat of blood. You are most welcome,
Command my house, and if you can affect
My Daughter, for whose love (as my Son here
Prepares me) you took this paines, I shall
Make equall propositions. I knew
Your Father well, Don Roderigo, who
Gave up his life with honor 'gainst the Moores.
Once more y' are welcome: Son Luys shew
The way to your Sister, and bid her entertain
Your friend with all the love her modesty,
And my commands may prompt her to.

ALBERTO
You much oblige my services.

LUYS
Remember Don
Conditions, if my Sister and you join
Your copyholds, I have a life must be
Maintain'd till the old man dye, hang his pension,
T'w'll not keep me in salads. I'le conduct you.

[Aside too, and exit with **ALBERTO.**

DON CARLOS
I like his person well, and his calm gesture
Speakes for his other composition.
The estate is competent, my Daughter is
Obedient, which rich Parents call a blessing,
Whose wisdom is to advance their name, and fortunes.

[Enter **DON RAMIRES**.

My Son is all my studie now.
My noble Don Ramires, you look cheerful.

DON RAMIRES
'Tis a good omen, I ha' buisness w'ee
Such as cannot despair your entertaiment;

You have a Daughter.

DON CARLOS
I would you had one;
I should be willing to translate a Son,
And by his marriage be most proud to call
Our Daughter mine.

DON RAMIRES
You are next a Prophet, Signior,
And but the Sexes differ, speak my thoughts;
'Tis is harmony on both sides; to be short
For let our gravities not waste time, and breath
In our affaires, give the Young leave to court
And spin out dayes in amorous circumstance;
My Son Fernando, I need not call him Heir,
His birth concludes it, I would commend
To fair Jacinta: 't can be no dishonour
To your Family to mix with mine.

DON CARLOS
Tis an addition
Will add a luster rather to our blood.

DON RAMIRES
'Tis my affection to you Daughter, which confirm'd
By observation of her virtue, makes
Me wish this tye between 'em; I may safely
Expect you will assure a portion that
His fortunes will deserve, who must enjoy
What I possess, unless you disaffect
His person, or decline his education,
Which hath not spar'd my coffers to advance him
In the best form of Gentleman.

DON CARLOS
I want
Abilities of tongue to answer this
Your freedome, and the bounty of your nature,
Towards my Daughter, and so far am from
Exception to Fernando, there's no Cavalliero
In Spain I wish to thrive so well in her opinion.

DON RAMIRES
T will be his encouragement,
If he entrench upon no others interest,
I mean not to except, how well he can
Deserve her nobly from a Rivall, if

Her heart be not contracted, this were to
Engage'em both to loss of Peace, and Honor,
Perhaps betray a Life.

DON CARLOS
You argue nobly,
She is yet Mistris of her thoughts, and free,
While her Obedience doth keep in trust
Her heart; till I direct it, which shall be
To love, and choose your Son to live within it.
Have I said home?

DON RAMIRES
You have. When they have met
We may conclude the Doury, and confirm
Our mutual assurances, till then
Farewell.

[Exit.

DON CARLOS
I like this well; Ramires has
A fortune for a Grande. Don Alberto
Must now excuse me, if my vote prefer
Fernando, whom my Daughter must accept
Or forfeit me. The new guest is not warm
In his access, and sha'not feel with what
Soft art, and subtle wayes, I steer her passion;
Yet were Alberto's state ten Maravides
Above Ramire's, I should place him first.
Fame is an empty noise, Virtue a word
There's not a Jew will lend two Ducate; on.
He is return'd, I must prepare Jacinta.

[Exit.

[Enter **DON RAMIRES** and **FERNANDO**.

FERNANDO
I hope my past life hath not sir so ill
Deserv'd, you should be jealous of my duty
When you command, although in things of this
High nature, man being nothing more concern'd,
Next the divine considerations,
Than in the choyce of her that must divide
The joyes and sufferings of his life, a Son
May modestly insist upon the privilege
That Love by his great charter hath conferr'd

On every heart, not to be forc'd, yet I
Freely resign my will, and what men call
Affection, to that object you present me.

DON RAMIRES

Apply your self then to Don Carlo's daughter
Shee's young, fair, rich, and virtuous, and I've had
Full treatie with her Father, who expects
Your visit.

FERNANDO

Young, fair, rich, and virtuous,
Four excellencies seldom met in one;
She cannot sure want servants, that commands
Under so many titles. I could wish,
(So much I have ambition to be thought
Obedient sir,) she were but one of those.

DON RAMIRES

She is all, and one.

FERNANDO

My duty were not less
If I forgave my self a happiness
To perfect your comands; sir, I am ready,
To try my fortune.

DON RAMIRES

There is no fear of thy repulse, and when
Thou dost confirm her gain'd to thy affection,
My greatest act, and care of life is over.
Go on and prosper.

[Exit

FERNANDO

He is passionate,
And like the fury of the winds, more loud
By opposition; such a providence
May be mine one day when I am a Father,
And he for whose advance my cares are meant,
Like me, may with a fair and formall shew
Disguise his thoughts too, yet I am to blame,
For my affection to a dream, a thing
With which my eyes only converst, to hazard
A Fathers love, and the rich peace it brings;
I'll uncreate the face I dote upon
And be my self, or—

[Enter **FRANCISCO**.

What? my brother?
Now Francisco, you met my father?

FRANCISCO
Yes, and he
Lookes as some newes had much exalted him.
You are not so merry in the face, what Is't?

FERNANDO
Nothing.

FRANCISCO
You held no controversies with him?

FERNANDO
No.

FRANCISCO
I cannot guess he was angry by his smiles;
How did you part?

FERNANDO
Exceeding kindly.

FRANCISCO
What changes your complexion?

FERNANDO
Th'art deceived.
Pre'the' how do men look that are in love?

FRANCISCO
Why? as they did before; what alteration
Have you observ'd in me?

FERNANDO
You have then a Mistris,
And thrive upon her favours; but thou art
My brother, I'l deliver thee a secret,
I was at St. Sebastians last Sunday
At Vespers.

FRANCISCO
Is it a secret that you went to church?
You need not blush to tell your ghostly Father.

FERNANDO

I pre'thee leave thy impertinence; there I saw
So sweet a face, so harmless, so intent
Upon her prayers, it frosted my devotion
To gaze on her, till by degrees I took
Her fair Idea through my covetous eye,
Into my heart, and know not how to ease
It since of the impression.

FRANCISCO

So, proceed.

FERNANDO

Her eye did seem to labour with a tear,
Which suddenly took birth, but overweigh'd
With it's own swelling, drop'd upon her bosome,
Which by reflexion of her light, appear'd
As nature meant her sorrow for an ornament;
After her looks grew cheerful, and I saw
A smile shoot graceful upward from her eyes,
As if they had gain'd a victory o'r grief,
And with it many beames twisted themselves,
Upon whose golden threads the Angells walk
To and again from heaven.

FRANCISCO

I do believe
By all these metaphors, you are in love;
I see you have a fancie, but proceed,
And be not melancholy.

FERNANDO

I have told thee all.

FRANCISCO

This is indeed a vision; you have
But seen her all this while, if I may counsell you
You should proceed, her face is nothing when
You have perus'd the rest.

FERNANDO

Tis dangerous.

FRANCISCO

You must excuse me Brother,
There can be no hurt in a handsome woman,
For if her face delight so much, what will

The enjoying of so sweet a pile of beauty?

FERNANDO
Thou hast infus'd a confidence, I will
Embrace this counsell, you shall with me Brother,
And see how I behave my self, the Lady
Is not far off.

FRANCISCO
Withall my heart, I'e pawn
My life you shall enjoy her; what is she
Of flesh, and blood, that will deny, when she
Is fairly courted? may I know the name
Of this lov'd Mrs? you may clear your thoughts,
I dare have no design to wrong your love.

FERNANDO
What think you Brother of the fair Jacinta?

FRANCISCO
Don Carlo's Daughter?

FERNANDO
To that happy coast
I now am sayling; we lose time, clap on
More wings thou feather'd God; thou hast put fire
Francisco into my drooping thoughts, and as
They had already bargaind with the wind,
They are aloft, and chide loves lazie motion.

FRANCISCO
A word before you fly; but is Jacinta
Your Mistris then?

FERNANDO
The beautiful Jacinta.
Dost think I sha'not prosper? what is she
Of flesh and blood, that can deny, when she
Is fairly courted? add to this my happiness,
That shee's the Mistris, whom, from all her sex
My Father hath made choice of for my courtship;
He hath already treated with Don Carlos,
And 'twas his last command, I should address
My present visit to her.

FRANCISCO
Very well;
If this be truth, you need not trouble wings

To overtake this Lady, to my knowledge
(I'm serious now) she has bestowd her heart
Upon a friend, who has already fortified
Himself against the world, that would oppose
His title to't.

FERNANDO
From what intelligence
Have you gain'd this? her Father knows it not.
Come, these are but subtle pretences scattered
By some, who cunningly thus hope to make
Themselves a victory, by cutting off
More fruitful expectations, this must
Not disingage me, prithee walk.

FRANCISCO
I can produce my Author, here, Fernando.
And with my blood defend that interest
She gave me, with intent I should preserve it.

FERNANDO
How, is she yours Francisco?

FRANCISCO
Mine, if hearts
Have power to make assurance.

FERNANDO
Tis some happiness
I have no stranger to oppose, whose high
And stubborn soul would not release this treasure
But make me force it through his blood. Francisco
And Fernando are two rillets from one Spring,
I will not doubt he will resigne, to make
Me fortunate; or should his will be cold
And some close thoughts suggest I had no privilege
By Eldest birth, but came a slie Intruder
Upon his right of love, there is a tye
Of Nature and Obedience to a Father
Will make him give this blessing from his bosom,
And strip his amorous soul of all his wealth
That may Invest my wishes.

FRANCISCO
I read not this
In any of the reverend Casuists;
No inequality being in our blood
The lay of nature meant we should be equal;

It was first tyranny, then partial custom,
Made you more capable of Land. Would you
Be lord of us, because you are first born,
And make our souls your tenants too? when I've
Nam'd you my Elder brother, I exclude
All servitude; Justice that makes me love you
Carries an equal law to both;
Nay I can love you more if I consider you
(Without the chain of blood) a friend, than all
The bonds of nature can enforce me to;
In both relations give me leave to love you
As much as man, but not resign my Mistris.
You ascend higher, and persuade by what
Obedience is owing to a Father,
They give us life, a good Son keepes it for him,
And every drop bled in their cause, a glory;
I can acknowledge this, and sacrifice
Life, Fortunes, a poor recompence to lose
(Were they all multipli'd) to shew my duty;
But these are things may be resign'd, a Mistris
Is not a wealth in ballance with the world,
But much above the poize of all it's happiness,
And equall with our honor, riveted
Into our soul, it leaves her not, when death
Hath toook this body off, but flies with it
More swift, to love it in the other world.

FERNANDO
You are very passionate.

FRANCISCO
I am very just,
And you shall find it brother e'r you twine
With my Jacinta, mine, if vowes may give
Possession of each other's soul.

FERNANDO
No more
May she be worthy of thy heart, till mine
Do entertain a treason to divide you;
But I, to satisfie my Father, must
Present my self, and trust me, will so manage
My love to her, as thou shalt have no cause
To Interpret me a rival. O Francisco
Our loves are of a kindred, for mine is
Devote to Felisarda, to her Cosen
Poor Felisarda.

FRANCISCO
Theodoro's Daughter?

FERNANDO
We never yet chang'd language, nor doth she
Imagine with what thoughts I honour her;
But here is the distraction, thou canst not
Expect more opposition from Don Carlos,
Than I must from my Father, if he knew
Where I have plac'd my heart.

FRANCISCO
Let us assist
Each other then, till time, and some kind caress
Mature our love.

FERNANDO
Let Fathers look at wealth, tis all their Saint:
Hearts are freeborn, and love knows no constraint.

[Exeunt

ACT II

SCENE I

A Room in Don Carlos's House.

Enter **LUYS** and **JACINTA**.

LUYS
How do you like Alberto Sister? is he not
A gallant Gentleman?

JACINTA
For what good Brother?
cannot Judge his Intellectualls,
But we have plentie of more proper men
In Spain.

LUYS
He is an excellent Scholar,
He was still Emperour in the Schooles, and since
He studied Logick and Philosophy,
He was the flow'r of's time at Salamanca.

JACINTA
Tis pittie he should be gather'd then.

LUYS
What be gather'd?

JACINTA
The flower you talk on.

LUYS
If you affect him Sister, he may grow,
And you may keep him still for seed please you.

JACINTA
And sell him out at sowing time to Gardners.

LUYS
Come, you must love him.

JACINTA
Ha's he the Black-art?
I know not how Magick or Philters may
Prevail, and yet he lookes suspitiously.

LUYS
You think y' are witty now, d'ee hear, you must
Affect him for my sake.

JACINTA
Now you speak reason;
I may for your sake dote upon him, Brother,
This is a conjuration may do much.

LUYS
Well said,
Thou art my Sister, this good nature shews it.
And now I'le tell thee, I ha' promis'd him
As much as mariage comes too, and I lose
My honor, if my Don receive the canvas.
He ha's a good estate, and I have borrow'd
Considerable monies of him Sister,
Peeces of eight, and transitory Ducats.

JACINTA
Which must be paid.

LUYS
Not if you marry him;

Conditions have been thought on.

JACINTA
How? conditions?

LUYS
And some revenue was convenient
To do things like a Gentleman, I may
Tell you, my Father is a little costive,
Purse-bound, his pension cannot find me tooth-picks,
I must live till he die 'tis fit you know;
Alberto ha's an Exchequer, which upon
Thy smiles will still be open.

JACINTA
Very good;
Then you upon the matter have sold me to him
To find you spending money?

LUYS
No, not sold;
W' are at no certain price; summes have been lent
In expectation, or so, and may again.

JACINTA
You deserve Brother I should hate you now.

LUYS
'Tis all one to me, so you love him;
For my part I desire but my expences.

JACINTA
What if another man supply your wants
Upon the same conditions of my love?

LUYS
I am indifferent, so I have my charges,
My necessary wine and women paid for,
Love where you please your self; I am but one,
I would not see him want that's all, because
My Father is not yet resolv'd about
His going to heaven.

JACINTA
Well sir, for Don Alberto,
You shall be his advocate no more, and there's
A Fee to bribe your silence in his cause.

[Gives him money.

LUYS
Why, thank you sister,—will you die a virgin?

JACINTA
Why do yo ask?

LUYS
I would speak for somebody, tell me but whom
You have a mind to, and I'le plead for him,
And if he be a Don he will consider it;
You may give me what you will, besides.

JACINTA
When I
Resolve, You shall be acquainted.

LUYS
But d'ee hear,
Untill you do resolve, I would lose no time,
Tis good keeping a freind, and a warm client;
You may look lovingly upon Alberto,
And let him hope at all adventures, in
Two moneths you may be otherwise provided
And he may hang himself, i'th meane time
Some favours now and then to the poor Gentleman
Will doe him good, and me no hurt, besides
You'l please my Father in't, whose vote is for him,
And that's a thing materiall. I am
To meet with Don Alberto, and some Gentlemen,
I will preserve his confidence, and tell him
I ha' talkd with thee. Have you any more
Of this complexion? cause I know not what
Occasions I may have to keep my credit
With men of mark and honour, where I am going;
You are my Fathers darling, and command
His yellow Ingots; tother Doblon D'oro.

JACINTA
So I may bring a rent-charge upon my self.

LUYS
The tother drop of orient mercie, come.

JACINTA
You care not what accounts I give my Father.

LUYS
Thou hast twenty wayes to cosen him, wedge it
Into the next Bill, he wears Spectacles,
And loves to read—Item for pious uses.
Can it be less to help a brother?

[**JACINTA** gives him more money

—Well said.

JACINTA
Let not this feed your riot.

LUYS
By no means.
I am for no Carthusians to day.

[Enter **DON CARLOS, FERNANDO, FRANCISCO,** and **FELISARDA.**

Farewell dear Sister—who is that?

JACINTA
My Father

LUYS
I cannot endure that old mans company.

[Exit

DON CARLOS
I am past complement, and must acknowledge
Your fair intentions honor us, she is no Goddess
Of beauty Sir, but let me without pride
Boast my self blest, Fernando, in her virtues,
And that which crowns em all, obedience.
Jacinta, Entertain this Gentleman
With all becoming thoughts of Love, his merit
(Out of no rash, but mature judgement,) hath
Prevail'd with me, to name him to the first
And noblest place within your heart.

FERNANDO
Until this hour I never had the confidence
More than to think of love, and hide a flame
That almost hath consum'd me. You may think
It worth a smile, and that I only flourish
To shew my vanity of wit or language,
But when you understand that I bring hither

No young affection, but a love took in
Long since at my ambitious eye, it may
Beget your gentle thought, or will, to cure me.

JACINTA
Pardon me, if the more you strive to print
A truth on this short story of your passion,
The more I find my self inclin'd to wonder,
Since you seem to inferre, You took in the
Disease at fight of me, I cannot be
So ignorant, as not to have receiv'd
Your Name and Character, but never knew
Before, when you did grace us with a visit?
And how then at such distance you contracted
A danger so consuming, is above,
My knowledge, not my pittie, if you could
Direct me to the cure with Virgin honor.

DON CARLOS
So, so, I leave you to the amorous Dialogue,
Presume you have my voice.

JACINTA
Sir, with your pardon,
You lead me to a Wilderness, and take
Your self away, that should be guide; do you
Engage me to affect this Don Fernando
In earnest?

DON CARLOS
Yes.

JACINTA
You did direct my love
To Don Alberto.

DON CARLOS
I dispence with that command;
You may by fair degrees, and honor,
Quit his addresses, and dispose your self
Mistris and Bride to Don Ramires heir.

FELISARDA [to **FRANCISCO**]
It does not thus become you sir, to mock
A Virgin never injur'd you; he is
Your elder Brother, I am here beneath
The level of his thoughts, i'th' nature of
A servant to my Cousin, and depend

Upon my Uncles charity.

FRANCISCO
May I be
Curst in my own affections, if I
Delude thee, though to achieve our best desires
We seem to dissemble thus before Don Carlos.
This is a secret yet to poor Jacinta.

DON CARLOS
You have my will; obey it.

JACINTA [aside]
Hath Francisco broken his faith already?

DON CARLOS
May you both joy, where you have plac'd your loves.
You apply close Francisco.

[Exit

FRANCISCO
With your good favour,
I fairly hope.

FERNANDO
Your Father's gone Jacinta.

JACINTA
I should be
Equally pleas'd if you would leave me too.

FELISARDA
This is a change.

JACINTA
Unkind Francisco hear me.

FRANCISCO
Tis my meaning. Brother I ha' prepard
Your story there with Felisarda; lose
No time.

FERNANDO
Jacinta, clear your thoughts agen,
And pardon that I took a shape to fright you;
I shall not grieve to see Francisco prosper,
And merit all your favours, since my hopes

Must thrive, or have their Funeral here.

[Taking **FELISARDA's** hand.

JACINTA
Are we
So bless Francisco? th'ast a noble Brother.

FERNANDO
I may suppose my Brother, Felisarda,
Hath made it now no secret, that I love you;
And since our stars have so contriv'd, that we
Have means to assist our mutual ambitions,
Do not you make their influence unprofitable;
Tis the first boldness I ere took to visit you,
Although my eyes have often with delight
And satisfaction to my heart observ'd you:

FELISARDA
You seem a noble Gentleman, and can take
But little glory to undo a Maid,
Whose Fortunes cannot bring you any triumph.

FERNANDO
How mean you fairest?

FELISARDA
Not to be flattered Sir
Into a sin, to cure my poverty;
For men whose expectations are like yours,
Come not with honour to court such as I am,
(Lost to the World for want of portion)
But with some untam'd heat of blood.

FERNANDO
I dare
With conscience of my pure intent, try what
Rudeness you find upon my lip, tis chast
As the desires that breath upon my language.
I began Felisarda to affect thee
By seeing thee at Prayers, thy vertue wing'd
Loves Arrow first, and 'twere a sacrilege
To choose thee now for sin, that hast a power
To make this place a Temple by thy Innocence.
I know thy poverty, and came not to
Bribe it against thy chastity; if thou
Vouchsafe thy fair and honest love, it shall
Adorn my fortunes, which shall stoop to serve it

In spight of friends or destiny.

FRANCISCO [aside]
My Brother
Knows my whole Interest in thee, to whom
My Fathers care directed him, but we
Thus mutually resolve to aid each other.

JACINTA
This must be wisely manag'd of all sides;
Parents have narrow eyes.

FRANCISCO
Our meeting thus
Will happily secure us from their Jealousie;
Our Fathers must not know this countermarch.

[Enter **DON CARLOS**.

DON CARLOS
Ha! I like not this; Fernando at busie courtship
With Felisarda, and Francisco so
Close with my Daughter.

JACINTA
Alas! we are betrai'd.

FELISARDA
My Uncle.

FERNANDO
You are her Kinswoman, and of her bosom,
I prechee in my absence, plead to fair
Jacinta for me; as an earnest of
My gratitude, accept this trifle from me.

DON CARLOS
Ha! 'tis a jewel.

FELISARDA
Without this reward
I should solicite sir your cause, and do
My duty to Don Carlos, who desires it.

FERNANDO
I take my leave.

FRANCISCO

Madam, I shall be proud
To call you Sister, but you will prepare
Another happiness if you vouchsafe
To speak for me to pretty Felisarda,
She's bound to hear your counsel and obey it,
If I may owe this favour to your charity.

JACINTA
Your goodness will deserve more.

FRANCISCO
I must follow him.

[Exit.

DON CARLOS
Do you take notice Felisarda, that
You live here on the bounty of an Uncle?
Your Father had but ill news from the Indies.

FELISARDA
Sir, as your goodness wants no testimony,
I shall attend it with all humble services.

DON CARLOS
How durst you in the presence of my Daughter,
Maintain such whispers with Fernando, Ha!

FELISARDA
Sir, he was pleas'd—

DON CARLOS
No more, I here discharge you.
Jacinta,
I'll provide one to attend you
With less relation to your blood. I'll hear
Of no defence, away—out of my dores.
Go to your Father Signior Theodoro:
His ships may rise agen were sunk by th' Hollander,
And Fleet from St. Thome, he may prefer you
To some Rich Don, or who knows but you may,
Born on the Plumes of his estate, be made
In time a proud Condessa, so adios
Muy illustre Sennora Felisarda.

[Exit.

JACINTA

Thus have I heard a tall ship has been wrack'd
By some strange gust within the Bay: his passion
Admits of no dispute. O my poor Cose,
I fear my turn is next to be an exile,
Thy absence must deprive me of Francisco,
Who can no more glad his Jacintas eyes,
With a pretence to visit thee.

FELISARDA
Tis not
My fear to suffer want so much afflicts me,
As that I must lose you, but he returns.

[Enter **DON CARLOS** with a Letter, and **SERVANT**.

DON CARLOS
Don Pedro de Fuente Calada coming hither,
With Don Alberto, and my Son?

SERVANT
Yes sir, the Count desires to see Jacinta
Whom your Son has so commended, and sent me
To give you notice.

[Exit **SERVANT**.

DON CARLOS
Ha! Jacinta, retire
To your closet, and put on your richest Jewels,
A Count is come to visit you; Felisarda
There may be some more art us'd in her dress,
To take the eyes of greatness.

JACINTA
Sir you speak
As I were meant for sacrifice, or sale;
The Count Don Pedro—

DON CARLOS
No reply; be careful,
And humble in your office Felisarda,
And you may live, and eat here, till Jacinta
Provide another servant to attend her,
Which may be three whole dayes; my anger is
Not everlasting; bid my Wife come to me.

[Exeunt **JACINTA** and **FELISARDA**.

[Enter **ALSIMIRA**.

I expect an honourable guest, the Count Don Pedro,
To see our Daughter, whom I have commanded
To appear with all her riches to attract him.

ALSIMIRA
If his Intents be honourable, I have heard
Don Pedro loves a hansom Donna.

DON CARLOS
He had better cool his hot blood i'the frozen
Sea, and rise thence a rock of Adamant
To draw more wonder to the North, than but
Attempt to wrong her chastity.

[Enter **DON PEDRO**, **LUYS** and **ALBERTO**.

This from Don Pedro is an honor binds
The service of our lives.

DON PEDRO
Noble Don Carlos.

ALSIMIRA
If we had been prepar'd, we should have met
This grace with more becoming Entertainment.

DON PEDRO
Tis fair, and equal to my wishes,

[He kisses **ALSIMIRA**.

—She
Does smell of roasted Garlick; this your Sister?

[Enter **JACINTA** and **FELISARDA**.

LUYS
That is my Mother, here is Jacinta Sir.

DON PEDRO
She has a tempting shape, I now am pleas'd.
I use to kiss all; hum a pretty thing?

[Seeing **FELISARDA**.

DON CARLOS [aside]

I like not his busie eyes on Felisarda.

ALBERTO
You will be faithful to me?

LUYS
Who, I faithful? how shall I live else?

DON CARLOS
Son Luys.

[Takes **LUYS** aside.

ALBERTO
Madam.

DON PEDRO
Will you be pleas'd admit Don Pedro, by
The Title of your servant, to presume
Sometime to wait upon you.

JACINTA
It were pride
And saucy ambition sir in me, to think
You can descend so much from your great birth,
To own a name, and office so beneath you.

DON PEDRO
I that before thought women easie trifles,
And things which nature meant only to quench
High flames in man, am taken with this Lady.
Luys thou hast wrong'd the fair Jacinta,
Thy praise was thyn, and cold, Spain is not rich
Enough to boast her equall: and I love her.

LUYS
Oh she will be to proud to know it Sir.

DON PEDRO
Proud, she must be, whose eyes have such command.
She has a pretty servant too, Luys,
I like 'em both.

LUYS
How, both?

DON PEDRO
They will do well,

One for a Wife, the other for a Concubine.

LUYS
It will become your high blood.

DON PEDRO
Say I kiss
Her white hand, and present her with these Pearls?

LUYS
Your honor shall command.

DON PEDRO
Your Daughter has a most magnetick face,
And I pronounce her happy, your consent
Confirmes her mine.

DON CARLOS
There's nothing in my blood, or fortune, but
Don Pedro shall command. I was Propheticall?
Come hither Alsimira, wouldst imagine?
Hee's taken with Jacinta, and hath praid
Already my consent.

ALISIMIRA
Believe not all
That great men speak are Oracles, our Daughter—

DON CARLOS
If she be stubborn, uncreates her self,
Be you wise, and counsell her to this ambition,
Or thus I loose you all; ha turn away,
That Faery shees a Witch, the Count talks with her.

ALBERTO
I hope you hold me not Sir less deserving
Than when you gave me free access to plead
My service to your Daughter—if that Don—

DON CARLOS
Sir you too much prejudicate my thoughts
I must give due respects to men of honor,
Nor is it fit I should impose upon
The Freedom of Jacintas love.

ALBERTO
Y'are noble.

DON CARLOS
My Lord.

ALBERTO [To **LUYS**]
I do not like this Don.

LUYS
Th'art of my mind, I do not like him neither,
And yet the blackbirds in the bush, see what
present he would give my sister.

[Showing him the pearls.

ALBERTO
Did she refuse it?

LUYS
I never mean she shall, what wrong my friend?

[Embracing him.

Yet I'l take all, and let him hang himself;
If he would send his eyes, I would undertake
To carry 'em to the Jeweller, they would off,
For pretty toadstones. Have no fear, my Mother
Is for you too, you must fee both your Advocates.

DON CARLOS
Jacinta!

JACINTA
Sir.

LUYS
She takes her self much honor'd.

DON PEDRO
You oblige.

LUYS
Let me alone to carry things.
Be confident to trust me with your honor,
If it would pawn for any thing [aside].

JACINTA
I'm not perfect
How to neglect Alberto yet, and must I
Throw off Fernando, but new Entertain'd

By your command? the World will censure strangely.

DON CARLOS
The World will praise thy wisdom, & my care;
Or if some giddy tongues condemn what's good,
Must wee be servile to that fear, and lose
That which will make us Judges of their folly,
And damn it with a frown of state? they'r fooles
That dote upon those shaddowes, Idle talk,
The slime of Earth-worms, that doth shine to cosen
Infants, 'tis fit wee raise our thoughts to substances.

JACINTA
Let modesty and nature plead a little,
If I appear not found to Entertain him.
I may collect more strength by time and counsell,
And for your satisfaction dare profess
My Lord hath too much grac'd the low Jacinta
With a pretence so noble, but I should
Be held not worth his person, and too light
At his first breath of courtship to fall from
My Virgin strength, and give my self his captive.

DON CARLOS
I shall alow that ceremony; the Count
Makes an address.

[Exit **ALSIMIRA, FELISARDA**.

DON PEDRO
I must use thrift in my delight, my eyes
Are prowd, and must be taught by absence how
To value such a Mistris. I do miss the chambermaid.

DON CARLOS
It will become me to attend.

[Exit **ALBERTO** & **JACINTA**

DON PEDRO
Your pardon.
I'll take it for an honor, if your Sonne
Be pleas'd—but to my coach?

LUYS
Oh my good Lord!
So much I am your creature, if you knew
But where to match me, I would be your coach-horse.

[Exit **DON PEDRO** & **LUYS**.

DON CARLOS
So, so, Jacinta's starres do smile upon her,
'Twil be a match, were but my Son as fair
In expectation of a bride, I'd write
Nil ultra to my cares, he is to aery
And volatile, a wife would timely fix him,
And make him fit to manage my estate.

[Enter **LUYS**.

But he returns, I'll feel his pulse.

DON CARLOS
thou seest how near Jacinta is to happiness.

LUYS
I did some office in't, she may thank me.
I first inspir'd his Lordship.

DON CARLOS
Such a providence
To build thy self a Fortune by some brave
And noble mariage would become thy study,
And make thy Father willingly resign
His breath, with confidence to know thee wise
To govern what my Industry hath gatherd;
What think'st thou of a wife?

LUYS
I think little sir.
What should I do with a Wife?

DON CARLOS
Imitate me, and study fame, and wealth
To thy posterity. Have I with care
Acquir'd such an estate, that must not last
Two Generations?

LUYS
The way to make it
Last, is not to think of Wiving; for my part
(Sir with your pardon, if I may speak freely)
I had opinion once I was your Son,
But fearing by your narrow exhibition
You lov'd me not, I had a controversie

Within my thoughts, whether I should resolve
To geld my self, or turn a begging Friar.

DON CARLOS
A begging Friar?

LUYS
'Tis as I tell you Sir;
This last I fixt upon, and ha' been studying
Where I conveniently might raise a sum
To compass a hair shirt Sir,
To make trial before I thrust my self
Point blank into the Order.

DON CARLOS
Thus wild Sons interpret still
A prudent Father; but you may discharge
Your Jealousies, unless it be your own
Devotion to be chast, and live a recluse.

LUYS
For that I can be rul'd; I ha' not liv'd
After the rate of hating any women
But I can hear of Marriage, if it be
Your pleasure: but these Wives Sir are such tickle
Things, not one hardly staid amongst a thousand;
Beside, unless you finde one very rich
A man may cast a way himself, and get
A bundle of Beggeries, Mouths, that day and night,
Are open like Hell Gates, to feed; I would not
Hazard my Freedom, and the blessings Heaven
Has lent you Sir, upon a Wife with nothing.

DON CARLOS
Thy pension doubles for that word; in Earnest,
How much I like this wisdom; take this Purse,
I will have no account, and find me out
A wealthy Maid or Widdow but not ugly.

LUYS
No? not ill-favour'd Sir, if she be rich?
A little old or crippel'd?

DON CARLOS
I wo'not ha' thee
Mary a crooked, deform'd thing, because
She may have children—

LUYS

Not, unless she have
An Infinit wealth to make 'em strait sir;
I'le marry a witch so she have mony sir.

DON CARLOS

No, on no terms a Monster.

LUYS

Then I wo'not.
And now it comes into my mind, they talk of
A young rich Widdow, Donna Estifaniar,
What do you think of her?

DON CARLOS

Thou hast nam'd one
To my own desires, she lives a Widdow still,
But she has refus'd many brave Dons.

LUYS

No matter,
I like her sir the better.

DON CARLOS

She gives good entertainment.

LUYS

I will have her
If you but say the word. I wear a charm
To catch a Widow; but this Purse will hardly
Last till we finish, I must do things with honor.

DON CARLOS

Thou shalt be furnish'd like my Son; kneel down
And ask me blessing, I do long to give it thee.

LUYS

I have your blessing here.

DON CARLOS

Ile find thee out
Some Jewells to present thy Mistris too.

LUYS

'Two'not be much amiss, the Gold will go
The farther Sir.—

[Exit **DON CARLOS.**

I know not how this
Came about, unless Don Pedros coming to
My Sister ha' made him mad, & wrought this miracle.
How careful he was I should not marry one
Deform'd, I ha' chose the handsomest things thus far,
And I mary with a Witch at these years, let the Devill
Ride my wild Mare to death; and now I
Consider on't I wo'not have the Widow
For fear o'th' worst, yet I'll to her,
And make a business on't to keep the old
Mans Baggs in motion; this with some good
Husbandry, and no play, may last a Fortnight,
Tis very Gold: yes, it will pay some scores,
Maintaine my Negro, and a brace of Whores.
Now fiddles do your worst.

[Exit.

ACT III

SCENE I

A Street Before Don Ramires's House.

Enter **DON RAMIRES, FERNANDO**.

DON RAMIRES
How, no success? where lies the opposition?
Don Carlos equal with my self profest
His free desires, and to dispose his Daughter
To meet thee with all loving entertainments.
What can she argue to thy birth, or person,
Attended with so plentiful a fortune?
I must believe thy courtship dull and faulty:
When I was at thy years and spring of blood
I wound my self like air among the Ladies,
Commanding every bosom, and could dwell
Upon their lips like their own breath, their eyes
Doubled their Beams on me, and she that was
Of hardest composition, whom no love
Could soften, when I came with charm of language,
Her Frost would strait dissolve, and from her eyes
Her heart came weeping forth to woo me take it.

FERNANDO

Yet you that did with a Magnetick Chain
Attract so many, could possess but one;
I came not to Don Carlos house with cold
Or lukewarm thoughts, but arm'd with active fire
That would have melted any heart but hers,
Bound up with ribs of treble Ice against me,
By which I found there is another fate
That governs love, against whose secret doom
In vain is eloquence or force.

DON RAMIRES
So Obstinate?

FERNANDO
Nothing that I could say
In my own cause, could make her tongue or looks
Promise an expectation to thrive
By any after service, this disdain
I did resent, as it became my honor,
And now confirm'd against her pride, have thought
Of somthing, that with your consent, may tame
Her scorn, or punish it to her repentance.

DON RAMIRES
Name it.

FERNANDO
She has a Kinswoman lives with her,
Felisarda Daughter to Signior Theodoro,
A trade fall'n Merchant, Brother to Don Carlos,
This Felisarda
That now lives on the charity of her Uncle,
Half servant, half companion to Jacinta,
And fair, I would pretend to love, observe me sir,
And in their presence court her as my Mistris;
Me thinks I see already how Jacinta
Doth fret and frown.

DON RAMIRES
I like it well.

FERNANDO
To see her Cousin so prefer'd, it is
The nature sir of women to be vext
When they know any of their servants court
Another, and that love they thought not worth
Their own reward, will sting 'em to the soul,
When ti's translated where it meets with love,

And this will either break her stubborn heart,
Or humble her.

DON RAMIRES
But what if this pretence,
By such degrees convay away your heart,
That when Jacinta comes to sense, you cannot
Retrive your passion from the last, or say
Felisarda should believe you, and give up
Her heart to your possession, when you
Are by your first desires invited back,
What cure for Felisardas wound, if you
Affect her not? although I like that part
Of your revenge, I would not have my Son
Carry the hated brand of cruelty,
Or hear Fernando broke a Ladies heart;
But live upon his clear, and honest truth,
And if Jacinta have not valued him,
Find his own estimation in some other
By fair and noble Courtship; Virtue is
Above the gaudy shine of Gold; and if
My Son love where his honor cannot suffer,
The want of Dower, I can forgive.

FERNANDO
You now, read exc'lent charity, and like a Father,
It is the harmony I would hear, I chide
My fears that did suspect you would prefer
Wealth in a Bride; there is no beauty, or estate, compar'd
To that resulteth from the soul; I dare
Now ope this narrow Closet, and present
The name I love above the World, it is
Sir Felisarda, equal in her blood,
Within whose vertuous poverty
More Treasures are contain'd, than in those veins
Of earth, which open'd by our slaves, do bleed
Such floods of Gold into the lap of Spain.
Pardon my long concealment of her name,
T'was sin against your virtue, and once more
Speak in that blessed Language, I may hope
To call this Virgin mine.

DON RAMIRES
How long have you
Been taken with this female holiness?

FERNANDO
Before Jacinta was propounded, this

Took firm possession of my faith.

DON RAMIRES
Thou hast discoverd thy destruction, foolish Boy.
Was this your policy to be reveng'd
Upon Jacinta, whom my providence
Elected to preserve our name and family,
To doat upon a Begger? thou hast flung
A fire into my brain; either resolve
To perfect my commands, and, throwing off
That trifle thou hast prais'd, prefer Jacinta
To the best seat within thy hart, and marry her
Or live a stranger to me, and divested
Of all those rights, which nature, and thy Birth
Have flatter'd thee with hope to find; expect not
Alive, the stipend of a Groom to feed thee,
Nor dead, the naked charity of a shroud
To hide thee from the Worms.

FERNANDO
O, sir, call back
That murdering sentence, it were sin to let
This passion dwell upon you, nor would Heaven,
Whose eyes survey our frailty, suffer
So wild a rage possess you.

DON RAMIRES
Tis within thy own obedience to divert it.

FERNANDO
When you have heard what I can say more,
You will chide your fierce command.

DON RAMIRES
What Riddles this?

FERNANDO
Jacinta is already made anothers, and my force
Upon her vowes, can be no less than sacrilege.

DON RAMIRES
This is some new pretence.

FERNANDO
Sir, not to wast your patience, she hath given
Her self by holy contract to Francisco.

DON RAMIRES

Thy younger Brother?

FERNANDO
This I know will calm
Your fury, and those eyes that threatend lightning
With smiles applaud Franciscos fate, and praise
My disobedience.

DON RAMIRES
Franciscos Mistris?

FERNANDO
His wife confirm'd by vows, & change of hearts,
I had it from themselves, when either strove
Whose circumstance should credit most their story,
Her tear or his conclusive groan, to seal
Their marriage, but both were equal sir,
What curse had I deserv'd, that should divorce
This Innocent pair of lovers?

DON RAMIRES
All this talk
Which foolish thou interpret'st thy defence,
Hath but inlarg'd thy folly, and that act
Which in Francisco I commend, upbraides
Thy own degenerate baseness: shall thy brother
Who carries all his portion in his blood
Look high, and carefull of his honor aim
At fortunes, and with confidence achieve
His glorious end, and shall his Elder brother
Ingag'd by nearest tye to advance his name,
Lye beating in the common tract of guls,
And sacrifice his birth and expectations
To a cozening face, and poverty? instead
Of adding mon'ments, that to the world
Should be his living Chronicle, to bury
His own, and all the antique honors (he
Ne'r sweat for, but were cast into his blood)
Within a dunghill? thou hast forfeited
Thy birthright, which Francisco shall inherit,
Nor shall the loss of my Estate be all
Thy punishment; hear and believe with horror,
If thou renounce not her that hath bewitch'd
Thy heart, Felisarda, and by such a choice
I shall affect, redeem this scandall nobly,
Fernando from this minute I pronounce
Heir to his Fathers curse; be wise or perish.

[Exit **DON RAMIRES**

FERNANDO
Why does not all the stock of thunder fall?

[Enter **FRANCISCO**.

Or the fierce winds from their close Caves, let loose,
Now shake me into Atoms?

FRANCISCO
Fie noble Brother, what can so deject
Your Masculine thoughts? is this don like Fernando!
Whose resolute soul so late was arm'd to fight
With all the miseries of man, and triumph
With patience of a Martyr? I observ'd
My Father late come from you.

FERNANDO
Yes Francisco,
He hath left his curse upon me.

FRANCISCO
How?

FERNANDO
His curse, dost comprehend what that word caryes
Shot from a Fathers angry breath? unless
I tear poor Felisarda from my heart,
He hath pronounc'd me heir to all his curses.
Does this fright thee Francisco? thou hast cause
To dance in soul for this, tis only I
Must lose, and mourn, thou shalt have all, I am
Degraded from my birth, while he affects
Thy forward youth, and only calls thee Son,
Son of his active spirit, and applauds
Thy progress with Jacinta, in whose smiles
Thou mayst see all thy wishes waiting for thee,
Whilst poor Fernando for her sake must stand
An excommunicate from every blessing,
A thing that dare not give my self a name,
But flung into the Worlds necessities,
Until in time with wonder of my wants
I turn a ragged statue, on whose forehead
Each clown may carve his motto.

FRANCISCO
Will it call

His blessing back if you can quit your love
To Felisarda? she is now a stranger
To her Uncles house, I met one of his servants
Who told me on some Jealous apprehension,
Don Carlos had discharg'd and banish'd her.

FERNANDO
He could not be so barbarous.

FRANCISCO
You know her Fathers Poverty.

FERNANDO
And her Wealth of Virtue.

FRANCISCO
It is worth your Counsel,
To examine what you may preserve, if wisely
You could persuade your heart to love some nother—

FERNANDO
What was't Francisco said?

FRANCISCO
Whose equal Birth,
And Virtues, may invite a noble change.

FERNANDO
Do not you love Jacinta?

FRANCISCO
Most religiously.

FERNANDO
If you can but contrive your hearts at distance
And in contempt of honor, and your faith
Sacred to Heaven, and love, disclaim your Mistris,
I may be happy yet, what say? I know
Jacinta's Wise, and when she understands
How much it will advance, her charity—

FRANCISCO
Our case is not the same with your's good brother.
Wee have been long acquainted, to contract
Affections, if I understand, your loves
Are young, and had no time for growth.

FERNANDO

Do not wound me.
Tis false, by Love it self thou hast deserv'd
I should forget thee now; dost thou consider
Love, (that doth make all harmony in our soul,
And seated in that noblest place of life,
The heart) with things that are the slaves of time,
And that like common seedes, thrown into Earth,
It must have leisure to corrupt, and after
Much expectation, rise to name and vigor.
Love is not like the child that grows, and gets
By slow degrees perfection, but created
Like the first man, at full strength the first minute,
It makes a noble choice, and gains from time
To be call'd only constant, not increas'd.
Preserve thy own affections, and think mine
Noble as they, I shall suspect thy love
To me else; prethee leave me.

FRANCISCO
I'll obey,
And study how to serve you.

[Exit. **FERNANDO** walks aside.

[Enter **FELISARDA**.

FERNANDO
Ha! 'tis Felisarda.

FELISARDA
Turnd out like one that had been false, where shall
Poor Felisarda wander? were it not
To ask a Fathers blessing, I would visit
Some Wilderness, e'r thus present my self
His burden and his sorrow.

[Enter **DON PEDRO**.

DON PEDRO
Had you no relation to Jacinta pretty one?

FELISARDA
I was her servant.

DON PEDRO
Come, you shall be my Mistris; they have us'd
Thee scurvily, I will provide thee a lodging.

FELISARDA
I shall not use your bounty sir for that.

DON PEDRO
Thou art a hansom Dona, here's a Pistolet,
Meet me i'th' evening, wot?

FELISARDA
Where, and for what?

DON PEDRO
The where, at thy own choice, the what, thy honor.

FELISARDA
You are not noble.

DON PEDRO
Don Pedro will Embrace thy buxom body.

FERNANDO
You must unhand this Virgin.

FELISARDA
For goodness Sir,
Add not your anger to my sufferings.
Unhappy Felisarda.

DON PEDRO
Is she a friend of yours Signior?

FERNANDO
She is not for your sinful knowledge Don.

DON PEDRO
Baser los manos, adios Signiora. Diabolo!
My blood is high and hot, unless I marry timely,
I must seek out a Female Julap.

[Exit.

FELISARDA
Don Carlo's fear of you was my first error,
But I accept my banishment, and shall
Humble my self to my poor Fathers Fortune;
You will be sir dishonour'd to be seen
With such a walking misery.

FERNANDO

Thy Uncle
Hath plaid the Tyrant with thee, but lose not
Thy vertuous courage; how our stories meet
And challenge kindred in affliction!
Oh Felisarda! I do suffer too,
And for thy sake, thou shalt know more; til I
Salute thee at thy Fathers house, preserve
Good thoughts of thy Fernando, and accept
This little Gold, no bribe against thy honor.

FELISARDA
My best return must be, my Prayers.

[Exit.

FERNANDO
Farewell?
Tis not impossible my Father may
Retract his cruelty, and by time, and some
Discreet ways yet be wrought to like, what now
His passion wo'not let him see, her virtue.
How many Seas are met to wrestle here?

[Exit.

SCENE II

A Room in Don Carlos's House.

[Enter **JACINTA** and **ALBERTO**.

JACINTA
I love you sir so well, that I could wish
You were a Witch;

ALBERTO
A Witch, your reason Lady?

JACINTA
Then twere within the circle of your art
By some device to rid me of Don Pedro,
Or if you could by any spell but get
My Father disaffect him—

ALBERTO
A Witch? That's a way about, I were best cut his

Throat a little.

JACINTA
You 're much beholding to my Brother sir,
He still commends you; such an Advocate
Deserves his fee.

ALBERTO
Unless my cause succeed
He has been feed too much; your Brother, Lady,
Preserves a noble friendship; if I were sure
You would be mine Jacinta, I could tarry
Till your Father die.

JACINTA
But how can you procure
Don Pedro to have patience so long,
Whom my Father pleads for and prefers?

ALBERTO
There, there's the mischief, I must poison him;
One Fig sends him to Erebus, tis in
Your power and wit to spin out time, I may
Invent a means for his conveyance. Ha!

[Enter **DON CARLOS, ESTEFANIA**, and **LUYS.**

JACINTA
The Lady Estefania.

DON CARLOS
Welcome again,
This is an honour to us, where's Jacinta?
Salute this noble Lady. Ha! Luys,
Hast thou prevail'd already?

LUYS
I'm i'th' way you see,
She has not been observ'd they say to walk
So freely with some men that boast more favour.

[Enter **DON PEDRO**.

DON PEDRO
What makes the Lady Estefania here?
I like not their converse, this day is ominous.

[Exit.

DON CARLOS
Was't not the Count Don Pedro that retird?
What object here displeas'd him?

ALBERTO
Ha, ha, didst see the Don?

DON CARLOS
Preserve your mirth—I must be satisfied.

[Exit. **LUYS** and **ALBERTO** walk aside.

LUYS
I'll lay a thousand Ducats that my costive
Don has been tampering with my Widow, I
Observ'd (when I by chance let fall discourse)
How much he was an amorous servant to
Jacinta, she chang'd her colour and did make
Such business how my Sister did affect him,
That I may guess, though I make use on't otherwise
To the old man, to keep the pulses of
His Purse in play, she came to examine chiefly
How matters here proceeded; well, if she love him—

ALBERTO
She is thy Mistris.

LUYS
My Mistris? yes, but any man shall marry her.

ALBERTO
How?

LUYS
She is a Widow, Don, consider that,
Has buried one was thought a Hercules,
Two cubits taller, and a man that cut
Three Inches deeper in the say, than I, consider that too,
She may be cock a twenty, nay for ought
I know she is Immortal.

ALBERTO
What dost with her?

LUYS
Faith nothing yet,
And have but little hope, I think shee's honest.

ALBERTO

Do's she love thee?

LUYS

At her own peril, w'are not come to articles;
There is not wit in wiving, give me a whore;
But that I ow thee money, thou shouldst never
Marry my Sister neither?

ALBERTO

Not Jacinta?

LUYS

No, nor any other simpering piece of honesty,
If I might counsel thee, while any wench
Were extant, and the stewes inhabited;
Is't fit, a Freeborn Gentleman should be chain'd
Tenant for life to one? Hang marriage shackles,
Ty the Town Buls to'th' stake, we must have concubines.

JACINTA

Don Pedro was too blame, and trust me Madam
He shall find nothing here t' advance his triumph.

ESTEFANIA

You are Virtuous Jacinta; I presum'd
When I should land my sufferings on your knowledge,
You would excuse my unexpected visit.

JACINTA

My Brother has been Just in the relation
How he pursues my love, but I shall be
Happy to serve your Justice, and must tell
The noble Estefania, my heart,
By all that love can teach to bind a faith,
Is plac'd where it shall never injure what
Your mutual vows contracted; I smile not
With mine own eyes upon him, 'tis my Fathers
Severe command to love him, but this story
Cleer'd to my Father would secure us both.

ESTEFANIA

If any faith or service in me can
Deserve this goodness, cheerfully employ it.

JACINTA

I will be confident to use your Virtue.

[Enter **DON CARLOS**.

ESTEFANIA
I will refuse no office.

JACINTA
My Father comes most aptly.

ALBERTO
Ha! Ha! Ha! Have pity on my spleen,
I shall crack a rib else, ha, ha, ha!

DON CARLOS
You are very merry, Don Alberto; Son,
You may be of the counsel too, this house
Is mine I take it, I advise you would
Frequent it less.

ALBERTO
How Sir?

DON CARLOS
I do not like your visits,
And to remove the cause, my Daughter is
Already sir dispos'd, to one above
Your birth and fortune, so fare-you-well.
You understand, now laugh and pick your teeth.
Daughter—

ALBERTO
Did you hear this Luys?

LUYS
I, the old man raves.

ALBERTO
Must not frequent his house.

LUYS
Would 'twere in a flame, so his money and I
Were out on't.

ALBERTO
But thy Sister—

LUYS
Would be refin'd i' th' fire, let her burn too.

ALBERTO

My friend, if I have not Jacinta,
There are certain sums of money—

LUYS

I am not of your mind Don, the sums are most uncertain.
Come, you did laugh too loud, my Father is
A Stoick, but despair not; go to your lodging,
I'll see thee anon, and either bring thee money
Or else some reasons why I do not bring it,
We won't go to Law, I'll pawn the widow
Rather than thou shalt want; go say thy prayers,
And shew thy teeth no more, till I come to thee.
Now the business here?

[Exit **ALBERTO**

DON CARLOS

We have agreed Jacinta;
And he to morrow privately
Will at the Church expect thee; tis an age
Till I salute the Bride to this great Don,
Whose thoughts are wing'd t' enjoy thee, and resolve
No more delay, prepare to meet this Honor.

LUYS

To morrow? this must be crost.

DON CARLOS

My next ambition Madam will be perfect.
To call you by some nearer name; my Son—

ESTEFANIA

Is a most noble Gentleman, I know not
Where lives so clear a merit.

LUYS

Oh sweet Madam.

DON CARLOS

Jacinta.

LUYS

I have a sute to you.

ESTEFANIA

To me?

LUYS
Only that you would not dote too much upon me,
A gentle easie sober pace in love
Goes far, and is much better than a gallop; if you please
We may hold one another in hand, and love
This seven yeares, without sealing and delivering.

ESTEFANIA
With all my heart.

LUYS
You'll do me a pleasure Madam.

ESTEFANIA
You instruct well.

LUYS
This Courtship is not common.

ESTEFANIA
I confess it.

DON CARLOS
Son Luys.

LUYS
Sir.

[**DON CARLOS** and **LUYS** converse aside.

DON CARLOS
Let her not cool.

LUYS
And she do,
I know the way to heat her again.

ESTEFANIA
I will not yet reveal my abuse Jacinta,
And if you please to favor a design,
I have a plot may serve to both our happiness.

JACINTA
I'll obey.
There is a trembling in my heart.

DON CARLOS

You must not leave us yet Madam.

ESTEFANIA
You may command me.

LUYS
My Don so rampart, there's something in this pannier
Shall spoil your match to morow; Don Alberto,
When I disclose, shall worship me: be drunk,
Cancel arrears, and beg to lend more money.

[Exeunt

A Room in Don Ramires's House.

Enter **DON RAMIRES, FRANCISCO & NOTARIE**.

DON RAMIRES
'Tis most exactly done, and firm.

NOTARIE
I could,
Omiting or inserting but a word, or particle,
Trouble the whole conveyance,
And make work for the law till doom's-day: but—

FRANCISCO
Is't possible?

NOTARIE
You do not know the quirks of a Scrivano,
A dash undoes a Family, a point,
An artificial accent i't'h wrong place,
Shall poyson an Estate, translate your Land
In Spain now into either of both Indies,
In less time than our Gallions of Plate
Are sailing hither; but you are my friend,
And noble benefactor.

DON RAMIRES
There's more for your reward.

[Gives him money.

NOTARIE
I humbly thank you Signior. Su Criado.

FRANCISCO
Farewell.

NOTARIE
Su Servidor.

[Exit.

DON RAMIRES
This deed makes thee my Heir Francisco, and
Will like a powerful spell upon Don Carlos,
Whose soul is superstitious upon Wealth,
Win his consent to make Jacinta thine.

FRANCISCO
Sir, I cannot say my duty shall deserve it
Since nature, and religion, without all
This bounty challenges my best obedience.

[Enter **FERNANDO**.

DON RAMIRES
Away, thy sight
Is my disease.

FERNANDO
Your blessing sir I kneel for.

DON RAMIRES
What Impudence is this? wilt thou subscribe
To take off mine, thy curse on Felisarda?
For I do hate her heartily; disclaim
All promise, contract, or converse for ever,
I'm else inexorable.

FERNANDO
Sir.

DON RAMIRES
His eyes shoot poyson at me, Ha! he has
Bewitched me sure, what coldness thus invades me?
Ther's something creeping to my heart. Franscisco? Ha!
Possess this gift of thy Inheritance;

[Gives him the deed.

Convey me to my chamber, oh—Fernando,
If thou dost hope I should take off my curse,
Do not approach my sight, unless I send for thee.

FRANCISCO
Forbear good Brother; Diego, Roderigo!

[Enter two **SERVANTS**.

Your hands t' assist my Father, one go for his
Physician.

[Exeunt **FRANCISCO** and **SERVANTS**, bearing **DON RAMIRES**.

FERNANDO
This turn is fatal, and affrights me, but
Heaven has more charity than to let him die
With such a hard heart, 'twere a sin, next his
Want of compassion, to suspect he can
Take his Eternal flight and leave Fernando
This desperate Legacie, he will change
The curse into some little prayer I hope,
And then—

[Enter **SERVANT** and **PHYSICIAN**.

SERVANT
Make hast I beseech you Doctor.

PHYSICIAN
Noble Fernando.

FERNANDO
As you would have men think your art is meant
Not to abuse mankind, employ it all
To cure my poor sick Father.

PHYSICIAN
Fear it not sir.

[Exeunt **PHYSICIAN** and **SERVANT**.

FERNANDO
But there is more than your thin skill requir'd
To state a health, your Recipes perplex't

With tough names, are but mockeries, and noise,
Without some dew from Heaven, to mix and make 'em

[Enter **SERVANT**.

Thrive, in the application: what now?

SERVANT
Oh sir, I am sent for the Confessor,
The Doctor fears him much, your Brother says
You must have patience, and not Enter Sir;
Your Father is a going, good old man,
And having made him Heir, is loth your presence
Should interrupt his Journey.

[Exit.

FERNANDO
Francisco may be honest, yet me thinks
It would become his love to interpose
For my access, at such a needful hour,
And mediate for my blessing, not assist
Unkindly thus my banishment. I'll not
Be lost so tamely, shall my Father dye
And not Fernando take his leave—I dare not.
If thou dost hope I should take off this curse,
Do not approach until I send—'twas so,
And 'tis a law that binds above my blood.

[Enter **CONFESSOR** and **SERVANT**.

Make hast good Father, and if heaven deny
Him life, let not his charity dye too.
One curse may sink us both, say how I kneel
And beg he would bequeath me but his blessing.
Then though Francisco be his Heir, I shall
Live happy, and take comfort in my tears,
When I remember him so kind a Father.

CONFESSOR
It is my duty.

[Exit.

FERNANDO
Do your holy office.
Those fond Philosophers that magnifie
Our human nature, and did boast wee had

Such a prerogative in our rational soul,
Converst but little with the World, confin'd
To cells, and unfrequented woods, they knew not
The fierce vexation of community,
Else they had taught, our reason is our loss,
And but a priviledge that exceedeth sense,
By nearer apprehension, of what wounds,
To know our selves most miserable. My heart

[Enter **PHYSICIAN** and **FRANCISCO**.

Is teeming with new fears—Ha! is he dead?

PHYSICIAN
Not dead, but in a desperate condition,
And so that little breath remaines wee have
Remitted to his Confessor, whose Office
Is all that's left.

FRANCISCO
Is there no hope of life then?

PHYSICIAN
None.

FERNANDO
Is he not merciful to Fernando yet? no talk of me?

PHYSICIAN
I find he takes no pleasure
To hear you nam'd: Francisco to us all
He did confirm his Heir, with many blessings.

FERNANDO
And not one left for me? oh take me in
Thou gentle Earth, and let me creep through all
Thy dark and hollow crannies, till I find
Another way to come into the World,
For all the Air I breath-in here is poyson'd.

FRANCISO
We must have patience Brother, it was no
Ambitious thought of mine to supplant you;
He may live yet, and you be reconcil'd.

FERNANDO
That was some kindness yet Francisco; but
I charge thee by the nearness of our blood,

When I am made this mockery, and wonder,
I know not where to find out charity,
If unawares a chance direct my weary
And wither'd Feet to some fair House of thine,
Where plenty with full blessings crowns thy table,
If my thin face betray my want of food,
Do not despise me, cause 't was thy Brother.

[Enter **CONFESSOR**.

FRANCISCO
Leave these imagin'd horrors, I must not
Live when my Brother is thus miserable.

FERNANDO
Ther's something in that face looks comfortably.

CONFESSOR
Your Father sir is dead, his will to make
Francisco the sole Master of his Fortunes
Is now irrevocable, a small Pension
He hath given you for life, which with his blessing
Is all the benefit I bring.

FERNANDO
Ha, blessing; speak it agen good Father.

CONFESSOR
I did apply some lenitives to soften
His anger, and prevail'd; your Father hath
Revers'd that heavy censure of his curse,
And in the place bequeath'd his prayer and blessing.

FERNANDO
I am new created by his charity.

CONFESSOR
Some ceremonies are behind, he did
Desire to ne interr'd within our Covent,
And left his Sepulture to me, I am confident
Your pieties will give me leave—

FRANCISCO
His will in all things I obey, and yours
Most Reverend Father; order as you please
His Body; we may after celebrate
With all due obsequies his Funeral.

FERNANDO
Why you alone obey? I am your Brother:
My Fathers Eldest Son, though not his Heir.

FRANCISCO
It pleas'd my Father sir to think me worthy
Of such a title, you shall find me kind,
If you can look on matters without Envie.

FERNANDO
If I can look on matters without Envie?

FRANCISCO
You may live here still.

FERNANDO
I may live here Francisco?

[Enter a **GENTLEMAN** with a letter and whispers to **FRANCISCO**.

Conditions? I would not understand
This Dialect.

FRANCISCO
With me, from Madam Estefania?

GENTLEMAN
If you be Signior Francisco.

FERNANDO
Sleighted? I find my Father was not dead till now.
Crowd not you Jealous thoughts so thick into
My Brain, lest you do tempt me to an Act
Will forfeit all agen.

FRANCISCO
This is Jacinta's character
[Reads]
—Fail not to meet.
As you timely will prevent the danger of my rape.
My soul! Estefania can instruct you all particulars—
My service to your Lady, say I shall obey her commands.

[Exit **GENTLEMAN**.

FERNANDO
Is that an Inventory you peruse?

FRANCISCO
Fernando you must pardon me, there's somthing
Of Essence to my life, exacts my care,
And person, I must leave you, we may seasonably
Confer of things at my return. Jacinta!

[Exit.

FERNANDO
Tis clear I am neglected, he did name
Jacinta too, in triumph, and is gone,
Big with his glories to divide 'im there,
And laugh at what my constant love hath made me.
My heart is in a storm, and day growes black,
There's not a star in Heaven will lend a beam
To light me to my ruin. Felisarda!
That name is both my haven, and my shipwreck.

[Exit.

SCENE II

Don Alberto's Lodgings.

[Enter **ALBERTO** and **LUYS**

ALBERTO
Excellent!

LUYS
You'l give me now a general release
For all the sums I owe you?

ALBERTO
Thou hast blest me.

LUYS
I was born to do you good; about it presently
Now you know where to ambush, away I say
And get comrades: Jacinta and my Mother
Is all the carriage, you may know the coach
By the old womans cough ere it come near you,
She has a desperate malice to one tooth left
Still in her gums, till she has shook that out;
You wo'not need a warning piece, farewell.

ALBERTO

Farewell, why whats the matter? you shanot leave me;
Thy Mother wo'not know thee in a Visard.

LUYS

You must excuse me friend, I would Join w'ee
I'th' surprise, but that—

ALBERTO

What I prethee?

LUYS

I have extraordinary business, that concerns me
As near as life.

ALBERTO

May not I know'? thou art going
To the Widow now, thy Mistris.

LUYS

Tis a business of more consequence;
Dost think I would leave thee, and there were not
Such a necessity?

ALBERTO

For what?

LUYS

And there were no more Sisters in the World,
You must excuse me.

ALBERTO

Nay, nay, we must not part, unless I know
This mystery, some reason why you leave me.

LUYS

If you will needs know, there's a wench staies for me,
The toy I told thee on; farewell Alberto.

ALBERTO

But will you leave such business and a friend?

LUYS

Business! art thou a Gentleman & wouldst have
Me leave a Ladie I ha'not seen this three year
For business or a friend?
I must to her; if I had a heart
Ten Ton of Iron,

This Female Adamant would draw it to her,
I feel it going; I do tell thee Don,
There is no business so material
In nature as a wench, and if thou art my friend
Thou wouldst leave my Sister now in such a cause
And bear me company, I must be drunk,
And she must pick my pocket too, that is
Another secret when we meet together
That never fails?

ALBERTO
Why art thou desperate?
Dost not thou fear thy body?

LUYS
A wench is Physick
My body has been us'd too, leave thy prating,
And let me take my course.

ALBERTO
And you be so resolute—

LUYS
I must give you one advice before you go;
When my Sister's in thy custody, observe
The time and place, and things convenient,
And stand not fooling about ceremonies
But put her to't.

ALBERTO
Thou wouldst not have me ravish her?

LUYS
Yes but I would,
She's no Sister of mine if she cry out
For such a business, she has more wit.

ALBERTO
Was ever such a mad-cap.

LUYS
I'll not pray for thee.

ALBERTO
I sha'not prosper if thou dost.

LUYS
Thy hand, Ile drink thy health, & hang thy self.

Farewell.

[Exeunt.

SCENE III

A Room in Don Carlos's House.

[Enter **JACINTA** and **ESTEFANIA**, hooded and dressed alike.

JACINTA
You tell me wonders Madam, Don Ramires
Dead, his Son Fernando disinherited,
And young Francisco made his heir?

ESTEFANIA
I took
Franciscos word.

JACINTA
Tis strange.

ESTEFANIA
Your stars smile on you.

JACINTA
Yet I much pity the poor Gentleman.

ESTEFANIA
Busie your thought about your own, Francisco—

JACINTA
Hath promis'd not to fail?

ESTEFANIA
He waits where he can easily observe
How soon the coast is clear to visit you.

JACINTA
So, so, thus hooded
The day cannot distinguish our two faces,
And for your voice, you know how to disguize it
By imitation of my cold and hoarseness,
And when you come to Church—

ESTEFANIA

Let me alone, there I'll produce the Contract,
Which will surprise Don Pedro, and your Father,
To see me challenge him, I ha' prepar'd the Priest too,
Whose holy Eloquence may assist, how ever
This will give you opportunity to perfect
Your wishes with your servant, put the rest
To fate Jacinta.

JACINTA
I hear some approach, retire into my Closet.—

[Exit **ESTEFANIA**.

[Enter **DON CARLOS** and **DON PEDRO**.

DON CARLOS
Jacinta.

JACINTA
Sir.

DON CARLOS
Not thy voice recover'd?

JACINTA
A violent cold—

DON CARLOS
Count Pedro must salute you ere we go.

DON PEDRO
Impute it to devotion, that I make
Such hast to be within thy armes,
One kiss and I shall carry with me
Another soul, and count with Joy the minutes
I am to expect this happiness.

[Kisses her.

DON CARLOS
Jacinta you follow with your Mother in the Coach;
My Lord I wait you.

DON PEDRO
There's Heaven upon her lip.

[Exeunt **DON CARLOS** and **DON PEDRO**.

JACINTA
He has kist, and took his leave I hope.

[Enter **ESTEFANIA**.

I must owe all my happiness to you sweet Madam,
I had been lost without your art to help me.

ESTEFANIA
Love wo'not leave his votaries.

[Coughing within.

JACINTA
I hear my Mothers cough, I ha' finish'd
And you must act your part:

[Exit.

[Enter **ALSIMIRA**.

ALSIMIRA
Come. Are you ready Daughter? the Coach stays.

ESTEFANIA
I attend

ALSIMIRA
Don Pedro will cure your cold before the morning.

SCENE IV

A Street.

[Enter **FRANCISCO** and takes away **JACINTA** hastily over the stage.

SCENE V

A Room in Theodoro's House.

[Enter **THEODORO** and **FELISARDA**.

THEODORO
What duty Felisarda shall we pay

To Heaven for this last care of us?
Let not thy eyes,
Although thy grief become 'em, be in love
With tears, I Prophesie a joy shall weigh
Down all our sufferings, I see comfort break
Like day, whose forehead cheers the world; if Don
Fernando love thee, he is a Gentleman,
Confirm'd in all that's honorable, and cannot
Forget whom his own vertue hath made choice
To shine upon.

FELISARDA
Unless my Innocence,
Apt to believe a flattering tongue, see not
The Serpent couch, and hide his speckled brest
Among the flowers; but it were sin to think
He can dissemble, Father, and I know not,
Since I was first the object of his charity,
I find a pious gratitude disperse
Within my soul, and every thought of him
Engenders a warm sigh within me, which
Like curles of holy Incense overtake
Each other in my bosom, and enlarge
With their Embrace his sweet remembrance.

THEODORO
Cherish
Those thoughts, and where such noble worth invites,
Be bold to call it love.

FELISARDA
It is too much
Ambition to hope he should be just
To me, or keep his honor, when I look on
The pale complexion of my wants; and yet
Unless he loves me dearly, I am lost,
And if he have but mock'd me into faith,
He might as well have murdered me, for I
Shall have no heart to live, if his neglect
Deface what my affection printed there.

THEODORO
There is no feare of his revolt, lose not
His character. I must attend some business.
If Don Fernando visit thee, preserve
His fair opinion, and thou mayst live
Above thy Uncles pity.

FELISARDA
Will you leave me?

THEODORO
My stay shall not be long; the Garden will
With smiling flowers encourage thee to walk,
And raise thy drooping eyes, with hope to see
A spring like theirs, upon thee.

[Exit.

FELISARDA
Why should I
Give any entertainment to my fears?
Suspicions are but like the shape of clouds,
And idle forms i'th' air, we make to fright us,
I will admit no jealous thought to wound
Fernando's truth, but with that chearfulness,
My own first clear intents to honour him
Can arm me with, expect to meet his faith
As noble as he promis'd—Ha! tis he.

[Enter **FERNANDO**.

My poor heart trembles like a timorous leaf,
Which the wind shakes upon his sickly stalk,
And frights into a Palsy.

FERNANDO
Felisarda!

FELISARDA
Shall I want fortitude to bid him welcome? [aside]
Sir, if you think there is a heart alive
That can be grateful, and with humble thoughts,
And Prayers reward your piety, despise not
The offer of it here; you have not cast
Your bounty on a Rock, while the seeds thrive
Where you did place your Charity; my joy
May seem ill drest to come like sorrow thus,
But you may see through every tear, and find
My eyes meant Innocence, and your hearty welcome.

FERNANDO
Who did prepare thee Felisarda thus
To entertain me weeping? sure our soules
Meet and converse, and we not know't; there is
Such beauty in that watery circle, I

Am fearful to come near, and breath a kiss
Upon thy cheek, lest I pollute that Cristall,
And yet I must salute thee, and I dare
With one warm sigh meet, and dry up this sorrow.

FELISARDA

I shall forget all misery; for when
I look upon the World, and race of men,
I find 'em proud, and all so unacquainted
With pity to such miserable things
As poverty hath made us, that I must
Conclude you sent from Heaven.

FERNANDO

Oh do not Flatter
Thy self poor Felisarda; I'm Mortal,
The life I bear about me is not mine,
But borrow'd to come to thee once again,
And ere I go, to clear how much I love thee—
But first I have a story to deliver,
A tale will make thee sad, but I must tell it,
There is one dead that lov'd thee not.

FELISARDA

One dead
That lov'd not me? this carries sir in nature
No killing sound; I shall be sad to know
I did deserve an Enemy, or he want
A Charity at death.

FERNANDO

Thy cruell Enemy,
And my best friend, hath took Eteranl leave
And 's gone, to heaven I hope, excuse my tears,
It is a tribute I must pay his memory,
For I did love my Father.

FELISARDA

Ha! your Father?

FERNANDO

Yes Felisarda, he is gone, that in
The morning promis'd many years, but death
Hath in few hours made him as stiff, as all
The winds, and winter, had thrown cold upon him,
And whisper'd him to marble.

FELISARDA

Now trust me,
My heart weeps for him, but I understand
Not how I was concern'd in his displeasure;
And in such height as you profess.

FERNANDO
He did
Command me on his blessing to forsake thee;
Was't not a cruel precept, to inforce
The soul, and curse his Son for honest love?

FELISARDA
This is a wound indeed.

FERNANDO
But not so mortal;
For his last breath was Balsam pour'd upon it,
By which he did reverse his malediction;
And I that groan'd beneath the weight of that
Anathema, sunk almost to despair,
Where night and heavy shades hung round about me,
Found my self rising like the morning Star
To view the World.

FELISARDA
Never I hope to be
Eclis'd agen.

FERNANDO
This was a welcome blessing.

FELISARDA
Heaven had a care of both; my joys are mighty.
Vouchsafe me sir your pardon if I blush
And say I love, but rather than the peace
That should preserve your bosom, suffer for
My sake, 'twere better I were dead.

FERNANDO
No, live.
And live for ever happy, thou deserved'st it.
It is Fernando doth make hast to sleep
In his forgotten dust.

FELISARDA
Those accents did
Not sound so cheerfully.

FERNANDO
Dost love me?

FELISARDA
Sir?

FERNANDO
Do not, I prethee do not, I am lost,
Alas I am no more Fernando, there
Is nothing but the Empty name of him
That did betray thee, place a guard about
Thy heart betime, I am not worth this sweetness.

FELISARDA
Did not Fernando speak all this? alas
He knew that I was poor before, and needed not
Despise me now for that.

FERNANDO
Desert me goodness
When I upbraid thy wants. 'Tis I am poor,
For I ha' not a stock in all the World
Of so much dust, as would contrive one narrow
Cabin to shroud a worm; my dying Father
Hath given away my Birthright to Francisco,
I'm disinherited, thrown out of all,
But the small Earth I borrow, thus to walk on;
And having nothing left, I come to kiss thee,
And take my everlasting leave of thee too.
Farewell, this will persuade thee to consent
To my Eternal absence.

FELISARDA
I must beseech you stay a little sir,
And clear my faith. Hath your displeased Father
Depriv'd you then of all, and made Francisco
The Lord of your Inheritance, without hope
To be repair'd in Fortune?

FERNANDO
'Tis sad truth.

FELISARDA
This is a happiness I did not look for.

FERNANDO
A happiness?

FELISARDA

Yes Sir, a happiness.

FERNANDO

Can Felisarda take delight to hear
What hath undone her servant?

FELISARDA

Heaven avert it.
But 'tis not worth my grief to be assur'd
That this will bring me nearer now to him
Whom I most honor of the World; and tis
My pride, if you exceed me not in Fortune,
That I can boast my heart, as high, and rich,
With noble flame, and every way your equal,
And if you be as poor as I Fernando,
I can deserve you now, and love you more
Than when your expectation carried all
The pride and blossoms of the spring upon it.

FERNANDO

Those shadows will not feed more than our fancies;
Two poverties will keep but a thin table;
And while wee dream of this high nourishment,
Wee do but starve more gloriously.

FELISARDA

'Tis ease.
And wealth first taught us art to surfet by;
Nature is wise, not costly, and will spread
A table for us in the Wilderness;
And the kind Earth keep us alive, and healthful,
With what her bosom doth invite us to;
The brooks, not there suspected as the Wine
That sometime Princes quaff, are all transparent,
And with their pretty murmurs call to taste 'em.
In every tree a Chorister to sing
Health to our loves, our lives shall there be free
As the first knowledge was from sin, and all
Our dreams as Innocent.

FERNANDO

Oh Felisarda?
If thou didst own less Virtue, I might prove
Unkind and marry thee, but being so rich
In goodness, it becomes me not to bring
One that is poor, in every worth, to wast
So excellent a Dower, be free, and meet

One that hath Wealth to cherish it, I shall
Undo thee quite, but pray for me, as I,
That thou mayst change for a more happy Bridgeroom;
I dare as soon be guilty of my death,
As make thee miserable by expecting me.
Farwell, and do not wrong my soul, to think
That any storm could separate us two,
But that I have no fortune now to serve thee.

FELISARDA
This will be no exception sir, I hope,
When wee are both dead, yet our bodies may
Be cold, and strangers in the Winding sheet;
We shall be married when our spirits meets.

[Exeunt.

ACT V

SCENE I

An Open Space Before a Church.

Enter **DON CARLOS**, **DON PEDRO**.

DON PEDRO
Your daughter does not use me well Don Carlos.

DON CARLOS
I know not what to think,
Some great misfortune must be the cause.

DON PEDRO
Not yet appear? they might,
And they had crept like Tortoises, Ariv'd
Before this time.

DON CARLOS
There is some strange disaster.

DON PEDRO
The Coach oe'rthrown, and both their lives
Endanger'd, can but excuse 'm.

[Enter **ALSIMIRA**, hastily

Oh my Lord, Don Carlos.

DON PEDRO
The Tragic voice of women stricks mine eare.

DON CARLOS
Alsimira?

DON PEDRO
Madam.

DON CARLOS
Where is our Daughter?

ALSIMIRA
My fear almost distracts me, she is gone,
Stolen, ravish'd from me.

DON PEDRO
Ha!

ALSIMIRA
An armed Troop
In Visards forc'd her from my coach; and heaven
Knows where they have hurried the poor Jacinta.

DON CARLOS
A troop of armed Devils.

DON PEDRO
Let them be
A legion, they are all damn'd.

ALSIMIRA
Nay they were men and mortal sure.

DON PEDRO
I w'on'ot leave one soul amongst them all.

DON CARLOS
Mine is in torment.
I'th' hope and height of my ambition
To be thus cros'd! how scap'd you?

ALSIMIRA
Alas I was not young enough, I offer'd
My self to bear her company, and suffer
As much as she did, but one boisterous fellow

With a starch'd voice, and a worse vizard, took me
Just here above my Sciatica, and quoited me
Into the coach agen upon my head,
I had a larum in't for half an hour,
And so I scap'd with life.

DON PEDRO
Did they sue her with any rigor?

ALSIMIRA
To say truth they were gentle enough to her.

DON PEDRO
That mollifies and they may live.

DON CARLOS
Hell overtake 'em, lets return, they had better
Committed incest, than this rape.

DON PEDRO
They had better ravish'd Proserpine before
Don Lucifer's own face. I am all fury.

[Exeunt.

SCENE II

A Street.

[Enter **ALBERTO** and **ESTEFANIA**.

ALBERTO
Pardon my dear Jacinta, It was love
That threw me on this act, I had no patience
To see thee forc'd into a marriage
By a covetous Father, whose devotion
Is only Wealth and Title; I esteem
No danger, if at last the fair Jacinta
Smile and allow this duty; let not silence
Deprive me longer of thy voice, whose every
Accent will please, though it pronounce my sentence;
There's death in this Eclipses too, sweet dismiss
Thy ungentle veil, and let thy eyes make bright
This melancholy air, that droops and dies
For want of thy restoring beams.

ESTEFANIA
Now sir,

[Takes off her veil.

What think you of your Mistris?

ALBERTO
You are the Lady Estefania I take it.

ESTEFANIA
Yes, you did take me from the coach Alberto
But by a consequence I find, you thought
Jacinta in your power, I could have told you,
Had you discover'd sooner what you were,
Where to have found your Mistris, but she's now
Above your hope, and by the priest ere this
Made wife to Don Francisco.

ALBERTO
To Don Pedro?

ESTEFANIA
It was not sir impossible that I
(Had not your violence prevented me)
(By a plot between Jacinta and my self,
To take her place and person in the coach)
Had by this time been married to Count Pedro,
Whom I have power and Justice sir to challenge
If Contracts carry weight.

ALBERTO
Have I so long
Ly'n beating at the bush, and is the bird
Fled to Francisco?

ESTEFANIA
I should shew I had
A passion sir, and sense of this captivity,
But that I find 'twas error, and not will
Lead you to this; and your own loss now made
Irreparable, helpes to tie up my anger.

ALBERTO
Madam, I must confess a wrong, and dare
Submit to let your anger punish me,
For I despise my self, now I have lost
My expectation, and if you please

To think I had no malice in this act
To you, You can propose no satisfaction
I shall esteem a penance to repair you,
As far as my poor life, if you'l direct it.

ESTEFANIA
'Tis nobly promis'd sir. You shall redeem
In my thoughts what is past, if you be pleas'd
To make my stay no longer here; I have
No desperate aim to make Don Pedro yet
Know how to right me, or make publick what
Should bind his honor to perform.

ALBERTO
Was not Luys Madam entertain'd your Servant?

ESTEFANIA
I shall make known the story if you walk
But to Don Carlos House.

ALBERTO
You shall command me.

[Exeunt.

SCENE III

A Room in Don Carlos's House.

[Enter **DON CARLOS, ALSIMIRA,** and **SERVANT.**

DON CARLOS
No news yet of Jacinta?

ALSIMIRA
None.

DON CARLOS
He must
Not live in Spain, nor in the World, if my
Revenge can overtake him, that has stoln
My Daughter; could you not by voice or habit
Guess at the ravisher? Ye are traitors all.

ALSIMIRA
Now I consider better, I suspect

Alberto one of the conspiracie,
Some voice did sound like his. You know he lov'd her.

DON CARLOS
Ha! Alberto?

ALSIMIRA
And how he might engage some Ruffians
To cross Don Pedro.

DON CARLOS
'Twas he, where's Luys?
I do not like his absence, thei'r both guilty;
My own blood turned a rebel? send for the Alcaides,
They shall both trot like thieves to the Corrigidor.
Where is Count Pedro?

ALSIMIRA
Gon in search of his lost Mistris.

DON CARLOS
When all things were ripe,
The very Priest prepar'd to seal our Ioyes,
A work my brain did labour for, and sweat
With hope to see accomplish'd, undermin'd?
And in a Minute all blown up?

ALSIMIRA
Have patience
She may be found agen.

DON CARLOS
But how my Lord
May be inclin'd to accept her foil'd, or wounded

[Enter **LUYS** drunk.

In fame—

ALSIMIRA
Luys is here.

DON CARLOS
Borachio, here's a spectacle! more affliction?
Where is your Sister, whats become of Jacinta?

LUYS
My Sister and Jacinta are gone together.

I know all the business.

ALSIMIRA
Where is she?

LUYS
She is very well, I know not where she is.
But Don Alberto is an honest Gentleman,
And has by this time done the feat.

DON CARLOS
Confusion—

LUYS
You think you had all the wit, it was my plot.
You may thank heaven that you are old, & ugly,
[to **ALSIMIRA**]
You had been no Mother of this World. But sir,
I have some news would be deliver'd privately.
Mother of mine, avant.

DON CARLOS
Th'art not my Son.
Was ever man so miserable? away
Thou spunge; get him to sleep,

ALSIMIRA
I dare not meddle with him.

[Exit.

LUYS
In sobriety
A word.

DON CARLOS
Where is Alberto?

LUYS
Where every honest man should be a bed, with my Sister,
Old man, I ha' consider'd o' the former mater we talk'd on
And would do things like a dutiful son, but I find that a
Wife is not altogether of convenient for me as a—

DON CARLOS
Will none deliver me?

LUYS

They are somewhat slug,
Now I have found out an excellent tumbler,
That can do the Somerset, please you to be acquainted with her, and give me your opinion,
She shall play with all the stews in Christendome, for all your are worth, if I live, and yet she is but
seventeen there's a periwinkle, I had a Gemini, before I went to travell,
And I am bound in conscience, if you think fit, to see her well Provided for—

DON CARLOS
With whips, i'll have her skin flay'd off.

LUYS
Her skin flay'd off? dost thou know mortal man
What thou hast said? I tell the Don, nothing can come near
Her in the shape of an Officer, she is a very Basilisk & will
Kill em with her eyes 3 score yards point blank, but you
May talk, & do your pleasure with her, for I came a
Purpose to bring her to your lodging, if you love me,
Do but see her, it shall cost you nothing, you shall
Be my friend, hang money?

DON CARLOS
Thus will my state consume, vexation!
What shall I do? when you have slept, Luys
I'l tell you more, attend him to his Chamber
And make his Door fast.

LUYS
You will consider on't, upon those terms, I will go
Sleep a twinkling.

[Exit **SERVANT** and **LUYS**.

DON CARLOS
And wo'not all this take a way my senses?
My Son is lost too, this is all a curse
For my ambition and my Avarice.

[Enter **ALSIMIRA** and a **SERVANT** with a Letter.

ALSIMIRA
News Don Carlos from our Daughter.

DON CARLOS
Ha! a Letter! 'tis Jacintas hand.

ALSIMIRA
Know'st where she is?

SERVANT
Yes Madam, and her resolution

DON CARLOS [reads]
To attend her Father, with my Master Don Francisco
If Don Carlos please to admit 'em, the matters done.

ALSIMIRA
What matter?

SERVANT
They are as fast as any Priest can make em.

DON CARLOS
Wife to Francisco, now his Fathers heir?
That's some allay, if it be true, she writes,
Don Pedro was contracted to Estefania, who supplied
Her person in the Coach—'t was not Jacinta was ravish'd
Then, Don Pedro was not noble, after he had made faith,
To intangle my Jacinta. Hum, say they shall
Be welcome.

SERVANT
They are present sir.

[Exit.

[Enter **FRANCISCO** and **JACINTA**.

DON CARLOS
I am nor yet collected, but if this
Paper be justified, I receive you both.
Peruse those wonders Alsimira.

JACINTA
Sir, though by the tye of nature you may challenge
All duty, this is done so like a Father
It exceeds all your care.

FRANCISCO
Let this confirme,
I bring a fortune not to be despis'd,
But were I Master of the World, I should
At price of all my wealth, think this a treasure
Purchac'd too cheap.

DON CARLOS
My blessing and my prayers, I'm new created,

And bow to that great providence; all Joy
Spread through your soules; this is not much amiss.

FRANCISCO
But what's become of Madam Estefania
That took Jacintas place?

ALSIMIRA
Forc'd from the Coach
By Don Alberto, thinking her my Daughter

JACINTA
That part of our plot fail'd, but my intents
Were fair, and to assist this injur'd Ladie

[Enter **SERVANT**.

SERVANT
Don Pedro sir.

DON CARLOS
You shall for some few minutes.
Withdraw into that Chamber, in his passion
He may be violent, leave me to moderate.

FRANCISCO
I shall obey you sir.

[Exit.

[Enter **DON PEDRO**

DON PEDRO
Was ever man of my great birth and fortune
Affronted thus? I am become the talk
Of every Picaro and Ladron, I challenge
A reparation of my honor; where's
Jacinta? tis a plot, a base contrivement
To make my name ridiculous, the subject
Of every scurrill language.

DON CARLOS
My Lord with pardon
Of your Altesa, y'are not Injur'd here,
Unless I have been faulty in too much
Observance, and desires to serve your person,
With almost sacrifice of my Daughter.

DON PEDRO
Ha! too much to me?

DON CARLOS
I would you had remembered
How much your Honor was engag'd before,
By Contract to another, when you mock'd
The Innocent Jacinta, now not mine.

DON PEDRO
Who hath traduc'd my fame, or mention'd me
With that dishonour? I disclaim all Contracts.
The unconfin'd Aire's not more free, than I
To all the World, except your beauteous Daughter.

DON CARLOS
Do you know the Lady Estefania?

DON PEDRO
Dares she make saucie claim? my breath dissolves it
If every Lady whom we grace with our
Converse should challenge men of my Nobility—

DON CARLOS
I wish my Lord you could evade it, for
The honor of my Family; if your conscience
Or Art can nullifie that Ladies sinterest
I am resolv'd—my Son Luys shall [Aside]
Then marry With that Widdow, I have no other
Ambition.

DON PEDRO
You are wise, and I
Am fortified to clear my self thought-free
Enter Alberto, Estefania with a Letter.
From any promise to that sullen Madam.

[Enter **ALBERTO**, and **ESTEFANIA** disguised as before, with a paper in her hand.

Ha! tis Jacinta, and she wears the Jewell
I did present, conspicuously; I ask
No reason for thy absence, let me chain
My darling in this amorous curl, tis happiness
Enough to repossess thee, not the policie
And power of Hell shall separate us agen.

ESTEFANIA
It is but Justice sir?

[Uncovering her face.

DON PEDRO
Ha! Estefania.

ALBERTO
Do you know her sir?

ESTEFANIA
Do You know this character?

[Showing him the paper.

DON PEDRO
Conspiracy.

ESTEFANIA
When this is read Don Carlos
You will imagine he has wrong'd your Daughter.

DON CARLOS
Is this your hand Count Pedro?

DON PEDRO
Mine—tis counterfeit
Upon my honor, and I thus dissolve
Thy insolent claim.

[Tears the paper

ESTEFANIA
Nothing can bind I see
A false heart

DON CARLOS
This must give you freedom Madam,
If you release his hasty vow.

ESTEFANIA
Faith cannot
Be compell'd sir.

DON PEDRO
These are all Impostures;
I take my self into my self.

ALBERTO

What shall become of her my noble Count?

DON PEDRO
I pity her
But cannot cure her wound, and if you be
Her friend, advice her to contain her passions,
And wisely love one that can entertain it.

ALBERTO
You hear this Madam?

ESTEFANIA
And can smile upon
His violated faith.

DON CARLOS
Now for Luys,
To strike in with the Widow,

SERVANT
He's a sleep.

DON CARLOS
I'll wake and quicken him.

[Exit.

ESTEFANIA
Hadst thou bin worth my love, I should have held
Thee worth my anger shadow, of a Lord.
Thy greatness I despise, and think thee now
Too poor for my revenge, and freely give
Thee back thy barren promises, and when
I read in story, one that has been perjur'd,
I'll write Don Pedro in the place of him
That brok his faith, and thank my fate t' have mist thee.

ALBERTO
If you please Madam, while he is i'th' humor
Of being base, I'll make him gather up
These paper reliques, which he shall make him self
Up into rolls, and having swallowed 'em
For Pills, thank you, his Physick was so gentle.

ESTEFANIA
It will be too much time & breath lost on him.

ALBERTO

It will become me Madam to attend you.

[Exit **ESTEFANIA**

DON PEDRO
So, she is taken off' and my path free
To Carlos Daughter.

[Enter **DON CARLOS** and **LUYS**.

LUYS
Contracted to Don Pedro? say.

DON CARLOS
She was, where is Estefania?

DON PEDRO
Gone with Alberto; proud to wait upon
The Lady I neglected.

DON CARLOS
Follow 'em Luys?
I do not like he should insinuate
Now she is free, and his hopes desperate in
Jacintas love.

LUYS
How long have I slept sir?

DON CARLOS
Thou dost dream still, persue the Widow now
Or never look at such a fortune.

LUYS
Is she gone with Alberto? what if I say,
I have lain with her, and that shee's with child by me?

DON CARLOS
That would stain both your fames; away and welcome
When thou return'st, and she confirm'd.

LUYS
Ile confirm her, or confound somebody,
No more, I am awake, this is Don Pedro
I'll talk with him first, will you justefie,
The Widow is a Widow still, and sweet
For all your Contract, that you have not been
My rival as they say after the flesh,

And that you did not know I had a mind,
Or not a mind, to do the deed of Matrimony?

DON PEDRO
Not I upon my honor.

LUYS
You are witness—now to Alberto.

DON CARLOS
Manage the business temperately.

LUYS
Let me alone to be temperate, if I do not cosen
Some body, let me never drink Sack agen.

[Exit.

DON CARLOS
What think you of Jacinta now my Lord?

DON PEDRO
As on the Saint I pay my chief devotions.

[Enter **FERNANDO**, with his sword drawn.

FERNANDO
I come to seek one, that I late call'd Brother,
But he hath forfeted that Name, and Justice
Weary of such a prodigy in nature
Hath arm'd me thus in he revenge, Don Carlos,
Obscure him not, no darkness can protect him,
My sword shall forrage every room like lightning,
No Cave but it shall visit, and through ribs
Of steel compel my passage to his heart,
Although I meet him in his Mistris Armes,
The lovers Sanctuary, I dare force Francisco,
And with my Sword cut the Embrace that chains him,
Rather then he shall glory in my ruins,
And revel out, those honors, with her, he
Took from my blood.

[Enter **FRANCISCO** with a Parchment in his hand.

FRANCISCO
It shall not need Fernando.

DON PEDRO

Hum, here is like to be a bloody business,
I'll not disturb 'em.

[Exit.

DON CARLOS
As you are Brothers, by your Fathers dust
That should sleep quiet in his Urne, by her
Dear name that gave you life, that now prayes for you,
Chide this unnatural furie.

FRANCISCO
What demands
Fernando?

FERNANDO
My inheritance wrought from me
By thy sly creeping to supplant my birth,
And cheat our Fathers easie soul, unworthily
Betraying to his anger for thy lust
Of wealth, the love and promise of two hearts,
Poor Felisarda and Fernando now
Wither at soul, and rob'd by thee of that
Should cherish virtue, like to rifled Pilgrims
Met on the way, and having told their story,
And drop'd their even teares for both their loss,
Wander from one another.

FRANCISCO
Tis not sure
Fernando, but his passion (that obeys not
The counsel of his reason) would accuse me,
And if my Father now, since spirits lose not
Intelligence, but more active when they have
Shook off their chains of flesh, would leave his dwelling,
And visit this course or be agen: my Innocence
Should dare the appeal, and make Fernando see
His empty accusations.

FERNANDO
He that thrives
By wicked art, has confidence to dress
His action with simplicity, and shapes
To cheat our credulous natures; tis my wonder
Thou durst do so much injury Francisco
As must provoke my Justice, to revenge,
Yet wear no Sword.

FRANCISCO
I need no guard, I know
Thou darst not kill me.

FERNANDO
Dare I not?

FRANCISCO
And name thy cause, tis thy suspicion not Francisco
Hath wrought thee high and passionate, to assure it,
If you dare violate, I dare possess you
Withall my title to your Land.

DON CARLOS
How is that?
Will you resign the interest to such
A fair Estate, and wrong my Daughter sir?

FRANCISCO
Let him receive it at his peril.

[Gives the parchment to **FERNANDO** who reads it.

FERNANDO
Ha!

FRANCISCO
It was my Fathers act, not mine, he trembled
To hear his curse alive, what horror will
His conscience feel, when he shall spurn his dust,
And call the reverend shade from his blest seat,
To this bad World again, to walk and fright him?

DON CARLOS
I am abus'd

FERNANDO
Can this be more than dream?

FRANCISCO
Sir you may cancel it, but think withall
How you can answer him that's dead, when he
Shall charge your timorous soul for this contempt
To nature and Religion, to break
His last bequest, and breath, that seal'd your blessings?

DON CARLOS
These are fine fancies.

FERNANDO
Here, and may it prosper,
Where my good Father meant it, I'm orecome.
Forgive me, and enjoy it, I may find
Some Earth that is not thine, where I may dy
And take up a dark Chamber, love Jacinta,
And while I seek out where to be forgotten
Live happy, and dvide the spring between you,

[Going.

[Enter **DON RAMIRES, FELISARDA**, and **THEODORO**.

FRANCISCO
So, so, all's well agen.

DON RAMIRES [Coming forward with the rest]
Fernando stay.

FERNANDO
Ha! my Father and Felisarda?

DON CARLOS
Don Ramires and my Niece?

FERNANDO
Are they both dead?

[**FERNANDO** Kneels.

I dare kneel too, they do converse. Don Carlos
Do not you know that shape? 'tis wondrous like
Your Niece.

DON CARLOS
And that your Father, ha!

FERNANDO
How long hath Felisarda been a sad
Companion to the shades? I did not think
To find thee in this pale society,
Of ghosts so soon.

FELISARDA
I am alive Fernando,
And Don Ramires still, thy living Father.

FRANCISCO
You may believe it sir, I was o'th' counsel.

[Exit.

FERNANDO
It is a joy will tempt me, wish to live
Here, without more ambition to change
For blessings of the other World; and is
My Father willing that we both should live?

DON CARLOS
Men thought you dead.

DON RAMIRES
It lay within the knowledge of Francisco and some few
By this device to advance my younger Son
To a Marriage with Jacinta sir, and try
Fernando's Piety and his Mistris Vertue,
Which I have found worth him, and my acceptance,
With her I give thee what thy birth did challenge.
Receive thy Felisarda.

FERNANDO
'Tis a joy,
So flowing, it drowns all my faculties,
My soul will not contain I fear, but lose
And leave me in this extrasie.

DON CARLOS
I am cheated.

DON RAMIRES
Not so, what dower you add above that fortune,
Descends upon her by your Sisters Legacie
Francisco shall deserve, with a proportion

[Enter **FRANCISCO** and **JACINTA**.

Out of my state; live, and be happy both,
You shall not want a Father in my care.
Our children thus increas'd Don Carlos, 'tis
Our shame if we neglect 'em; Theodoro
You now may call me Brother.

THEODORO
I'm honor'd.

DON CARLOS
Well, take my blessing too, love her Francisco.
My bounty is to come, and if my Son
But finish with his Mistris—he's return'd,

[Enter **LUYS**.

Where is the Widow?

LUYS
Sure enough.

DON CARLOS
And Don Alberto?

LUYS
I have made him sure too, I have pepper'd him.

DON CARLOS
How?

LUYS
In your ear, I have cut his throat, do none persue me?

DON CARLOS
I hope thou hast not kill'd him? ha!

LUYS
You hope to late, I could not help it, you said
He was my Rival.

DON CARLOS
Not to loud.

LUYS
Where, where shall I obscure me, the Alcaides
Will be here presently, and search for me.
I left him giving up the ghost, at a cranny
I made into his side, through which a man
Might see into his midriff.

DON CARLOS
Art thou desperate?

LUYS
Beside one window that did look into his lungs,
From whence his wind came strong enough,
In six hours sail to dispatch a Carrack to the straightes.

DON CARLOS
I'm mad.

LUYS
I should neglect my life, but 'twould not sound well
With your honor that Don Carlos Son was hang'd,
Or put into the Gallies; are they not come yet?

DON CARLOS
I am undone, there is no safety here,
Make fast those doors, and by the Postern gate
Thou mayst escape, take the best Horse, away.

LUYS
I shall want money sir.

DON CARLOS
Come follow me?
This accident I fear will quite distract me.

LUYS
You must dispatch me quickly sir, there is
No staying to tell the money, gee't me in lump,
I'll count it afterwards, good sir make hast.

[Exit **LUYS** and **DON CARLOS**

DON RAMIRES
Something hath happened that doth fresh
Perplex him.

FRANCISCO
Where is Don Pedro?

FERNANDO
He's here.

[Enter **DON PEDRO**.

DON PEDRO
The storm is over sure, I hear no noise,
Toledos are asleep, Jacinta! have
I found my love?

FRANCISCO
Here 'twas lost indeed,
I must allow no such Familiarity

With my Wife.

DON PEDRO
How? married?

JACINTA
'Tis most true my Lord.

DON PEDRO
You have not us'd me thus?

FRANCISCO
It had been Impious to divorce your heart
From Estefania; My good Lord, wee know
Your Lordship is religious in your promises.

DON PEDRO [To **FELISARDA**]
I defy all Estefanias, Lady you are civill.

FERNANDO
It will become my care so to preserve her
My Honorable Count.

DON PEDRO
Honorable?
It appeares not by these contempts.

DON RAMIRES
Your Lordship cannot want a Female Furniture.

[Enter **ALBERTO** and **ESTEFANIA**.

DON PEDRO
I must have some body now I'm prepar'd, my blood
Will take it ill, would I had Estefania;
Shee's here, Madam I hope you have
A better faith than to believe I was in Earnest,
Don Pedro is only at your service.

ESTEFANIA
'Tis too late sir, this Gent. is witness,
Of your surrender, and is now possest
Of all that's mine.

ALBERTO
It was your Noble bounty,
For which I cannot study a return
More apt than to resign to your good Lordship,

My Interest in Jacinta, give you joy Count.
Such a rich Widow serves my turn.

DON PEDRO
So so,
If I consider well this is but Justice.

[Enter **DON CARLOS**.

DON CARLOS
Ha! are not you Don Alberto: fetch back Luys.

ALBERTO
The very same sir, and this Lady is my Wife,
Please you salute her.

[Enter **LUYS**.

LUYS
Sir for the credit of your wisdom talk not,
The man you see's alive and married too,
With my consent, alas I ow'd him money,
That Widow has paid all, I must be honest,
I had no heart to leave you so unsatisfied,
These sums must go for other debts,
My debts do clog my conscience, and are better
When they are timely paid sir, then let run
With their long Teeth to bite your state hereafter,
And if when I am free you dare but trust me—

DON CARLOS
Was ever Father cheated thus, come hither,
How darst thou be so impudent?

LUYS
I cannot help it sir, unless you dye
Or give me better means, I shall make bold
With these devices, you are my Father sir,
And I am bound—

DON CARLOS
To cosen me?

LUYS
All must be mine, and if
I pay my self a little before the day,
You shall be no loser when you come to reckon,
This sha'not make a breach twixt you and I,

They are honest men I ow this money too,
When I am clear prescribe me any method
And rank me like your son, I will deserve
You shall forget my wildness, and acknowledge me
A convert without blemish to your family.

DON RAMIRES
I must be Intercessor.

JACINTA
And we all.

DON CARLOS
I'll think upon't.

DON PEDRO
Since I cannot have Jacinta, I desire
I may have her Brother.

LUYS
Not in marriage.

DON PEDRO
I like his wit, his spirit, and his humor,
Do not you love a wench?

LUYS
Yes sir.

DON PEDRO
Thou sha't never want.

LUYS
Wenches?

DON PEDRO
We'll live together, and if thy Father
Be not bountiful, thou shalt command my fortune.

LUYS
You speak nobly.

DON PEDRO
Ladies, I ask your pardon
Unless you hold me desperate, disdaine not
That I may this day wait upon your triumph,
And to each Bride offer some gift to expiate
My folly and offence.

DON RAMIRES
You are too bountiful.

DON CARLOS
Y'are all my guests to day.

DON RAMIRES
I beg your next
Remove may place the Scen' of Joy with me,
My house shall be much honor'd, lead the way
With Verse and Wine let Poets crown this day.

[Exeunt **OMNES**.

EPILOGUE

DON PEDRO
So, so, your dangers over, and the state
Secure, as when our Fleet in Eighty Eight
Was fir'd and scatter'd, to confirm it true
Here is Don Pedro taken Prisoner too,
I'm at your mercy Gentlemen, and I
Confess without a rack conspiracy,
So far as my poor part i'th' Play comes too,
But I am innocent from hurt to you,
And I dare quit the rest from any plot
Meant but to please, if you believe it not
I dare make oath, your hands can do no less
Than certifie your friends what I confess.

FINIS.

JAMES SHIRLEY – A CONCISE BIBLIOGRAPHY

The following includes years of first publication, and of performance if known, together with dates of licensing by the Master of the Revels if available.

TRAGEDIES
The Maid's Revenge (licensed 9th February 1626; printed, 1639)
The Traitor (licensed 4th May 1631; printed, 1635)
Love's Cruelty (licensed 14th November 1631; printed, 1640)
The Politician (acted, 1639; printed, 1655)
The Cardinal (licensed 25th May 1641; printed, 1652).

The Grateful Servant (licensed 3rd November 1629 as The Faithful Servant; printed 1630)
The Young Admiral (licensed 3rd July 1633; printed 1637)
The Coronation (licensed 6th February 1635, as Shirley's, but printed in 1640 as a work of John Fletcher)
The Duke's Mistress (licensed 18th January 1636; printed 1638)
The Gentleman of Venice (licensed 30th October 1639; printed 1655)
The Doubtful Heir (printed 1652), licensed as Rosania, or Love's Victory in 1640
The Imposture (licensed 10th November 1640; printed 1652)
The Court Secret (printed 1653).

COMEDIES

Love Tricks, or the School of Complement (licensed 10th February 1625; printed under its subtitle, 1631)
The Wedding (ca. 1626; printed 1629)
The Brothers (licensed 4th November 1626; printed 1652)
The Witty Fair One (licensed 3rd October 1628; printed 1633)
The Humorous Courtier (licensed 17th May 1631; printed 1640).
The Changes, or Love in a Maze (licensed 10th January 1632; printed 1639)
Hyde Park (licensed 20th April 1632; printed 1637)
The Ball (licensed 16th November 1632; printed 1639)
The Bird in a Cage, or The Beauties (licensed 21st January 1633; printed 1633)
The Gamester (licensed 11th November 1633; printed 1637)
The Example (licensed 24th June 1634; printed 1637)
The Opportunity (licensed 29th November 1634; printed 1640)
The Lady of Pleasure (licensed 15th October 1635; printed 1637)
The Royal Master (acted and printed 1638)
The Constant Maid, or Love Will Find Out the Way (printed 1640)
The Sisters (licensed 26th April 1642; printed 1653).
Honoria and Mammon (printed 1659)

DRAMAS

A Contention for Honor and Riches (printed 1633), morality play
The Triumph of Peace (licensed 3rd February 1634; printed 1634), masque
The Arcadia (printed 1640), pastoral tragicomedy
St. Patrick for Ireland (printed 1640), neo-miracle play
The Triumph of Beauty (ca. 1640; printed 1646), masque
The Contention of Ajax and Ulysses (printed 1659), entertainment
Cupid and Death (performed 26th March 1653; printed 1659), masque

www.ingramcontent.com/pod-product-compliance
Lightning Source LLC
Chambersburg PA
CBHW060133050426
42448CB00010B/2097